INTRUSION DETECTION IN DISTRIBUTED SYSTEMS

An Abstraction-Based Approach

by

Peng Ning
North Carolina State University, U.S.A.

Sushil Jajodia
George Mason University, U.S.A.

X. Sean Wang
University of Vermont, U.S.A.

SPRINGER SCIENCE+BUSINESS MEDIA, LLC

Advances in Information Security

Sushil Jajodia
Consulting editor
Center for Secure Information Systems
George Mason University
Fairfax, VA 22030-4444
email: jajodia@gmu.edu

The goals of Kluwer International Series on ADVANCES IN INFORMATION SECURITY are, one, to establish the state of the art of, and set the course for future research in information security and, two, to serve as a central reference source for advanced and timely topics in information security research and development. The scope of this series includes all aspects of computer and network security and related areas such as fault tolerance and software assurance.

ADVANCES IN INFORMATION SECURITY aims to publish thorough and cohesive overviews of specific topics in information security, as well as works that are larger in scope or that contain more detailed background information than can be accommodated in shorter survey articles. The series also serves as a forum for topics that may not have reached a level of maturity to warrant a comprehensive textbook treatment.

Researchers as well as developers are encouraged to contact Professor Sushil Jajodia with ideas for books under this series.

Additional titles in the series:

Additional information about this series can be obtained from
http://www.wkap.nl/prod/s/ADIS

*To my grandma Huijun Wu,
and parents Changcheng
Ning and Kuiling Ao.
– PN*

*To my parents and my wife.
–SJ*

*To my children, with joy.
–XW*

Contents

List of Figures

List of Tables

Preface

Intrusions in an information system are the activities that violate the security policy of the system, and *intrusion detection* is the process to identify intrusions. Intrusion detection has been studied for over 20 years. It is based on the beliefs that an intruder's behavior will be noticeably different from that of a legitimate user and that many unauthorized actions will be detectable.

Intrusion detection systems (IDSs) are usually deployed along with other preventive security mechanisms, such as access control and authentication, as a second line of defense that protects information systems. Intrusion detection complements the protective mechanisms to improve the system security. Moreover, even if the preventive security mechanisms can protect information systems successfully, it is still desirable to know what intrusion attempts have happened or are happening, so that the users can understand the security threats and risks, and thus be better prepared for future attacks.

Intrusion detection techniques are traditionally categorized into two classes: *anomaly detection* and *misuse detection*. Anomaly detection is based on the normal behavior of a subject (e.g., a user or a system); any action that significantly deviates from the normal behavior is considered intrusive. Misuse detection catches intrusions in terms of the characteristics of known attacks or system vulnerabilities; any action that conforms to the pattern of a known attack or vulnerability is considered intrusive.

Alternatively, IDSs may be classified into host-based IDSs, distributed IDSs, and network-based IDSs according to the sources of the audit information used by each IDS. Host-based IDSs get audit data from host audit trails, usually aiming at detecting attacks against a single host; distributed IDSs gather audit data from multiple hosts and possibly the network that connects the hosts, aiming at detecting attacks involving multiple hosts; network-based IDSs use network traffic as the audit data source, relieving the burden on the hosts that usually provide normal computing services.

This monograph presents the research contributions in three areas with respect to intrusion detection in distributed systems. The first contribution is an abstraction-based approach to addressing heterogeneity and autonomy of distributed environments. Specifically, the concept of *system view* is introduced to provide an abstract interface between different systems. On the one hand, system views hide the difference between heterogeneous systems; on the other hand, they describe what information an autonomous system is willing to provide to other systems.

The second contribution is a formal framework for modeling requests among cooperative IDSs and its application to Common Intrusion Detection Framework (CIDF). The first problem is how to enable IDSs to request specific information from other IDSs. To address this problem, the proposed technique represents a request to an IDS as a pattern plus a transformation rule, where the pattern specifies the events that the requesting party is interested in and the transformation rule extracts interesting information from the events. The formal approach is also used to add a query facility to the Common Intrusion Detection Framework (CIDF), which allows an IDS to form flexible requests to other systems.

The third contribution is a novel approach to coordinating different IDSs for distributed event correlation. The proposed technique represents the event correlation to be performed as a pattern (called a *signature*) among distributed events. A decentralized method is then presented for autonomous but cooperative IDSs to perform the event correlation specified by signatures. Specifically, a signature is decomposed into finer units called *detection tasks*, each of which represents the activity to be monitored in one place. The IDSs (involved in a signature) then perform the detection tasks cooperatively according to the "dependency" relationships among these tasks. Our approach is superior to the existing centralized or hierarchical approaches in that (1) communication is more efficient by having different IDSs communicate with each other only when necessary and (2) no centralized or hierarchical trust is required. As an important application of distributed event correlation, this approach can be used to represent and detect distributed (or coordinated) attacks that cannot be detected from a single place. An experimental system called CARDS has been implemented to test the feasibility of the proposed approaches.

PENG NING, SUSHIL JAJODIA, AND X. SEAN WANG

Acknowledgments

We are grateful to Joe Giordano of the Air Force Research Laboratory/Rome, David Hislop of the Army Research Office, and Maria Zemankova of the National Science Foundation for sponsoring our research presented in this volume.

It is also a pleasure to acknowledge the Association for Computing Machinery for allowing us to use material from "Abstraction-based intrusion detection in distributed environments," *ACM Transactions on Information and System Security*, Vol. 4, No. 4, November 2001, pages 407–452, and Elsevier Science for permission to use material from "Modeling requests among cooperating intrusion detection systems," *Computer Communications*, Vol. 23, No. 17, November 2000, pages 1702–1715, and "Design and Implementation of A Decentralized Prototype System for Detecting Distributed Attacks," *Computer Communications*, Vol. 25, No. 15, September 2002, pages 1374–1391.

Series Foreword

ADVANCES IN INFORMATION SECURITY

Sushil Jajodia
Consulting Editor

Center for Secure Information Systems
George Mason University
Fairfax, VA 22030-4444

email: jajodia@gmu.edu

Welcome to the ninth volume of the Kluwer International Series on ADVANCES IN INFORMATION SECURITY. The goals of this series are, one, to establish the state of the art of, and set the course for future research in information security and, two, to serve as a central reference source for advanced and timely topics in information security research and development. The scope of this series includes all aspects of computer and network security and related areas such as fault tolerance and software assurance.

ADVANCES IN INFORMATION SECURITY aims to publish thorough and cohesive overviews of specific topics in information security, as well as works that are larger in scope or contain more detailed background information than can be accommodated in shorter survey articles. The series also serves as a forum for topics that may not have reached a level of maturity to warrant a comprehensive textbook treatment.

The success of this series depends on contributions by researchers and developers such as you. If you have an idea for a book that is appropriate for this series, I encourage you to contact me. I would be happy to discuss any potential projects with you. Additional information about this series can be obtained from www.wkap.nl/series.htm/ADIS.

SUSHIL JAJODIA
Consulting Editor

Chapter 1

INTRODUCTION

1.   Computer Security and Intrusion Detection

Computer security has been studied as a discipline since the early 1970s. It refers to *measures and controls that protect an information system against denial of service and unauthorized (accidental or intentional) disclosure, modification, or destruction of information systems and data* [Abrams et al., 1997]. Researchers have commonly summarized computer security as *confidentiality, integrity* and *availability* [ITSE, 1991]. Confidentiality refers to prevention/determent/detection of unauthorized disclosure of information; integrity refers to prevention/determent/detection of unauthorized modification of information; and availability refers to prevention/determent/detection of unauthorized withholding of information or resource.

Though different computer systems may have different security policies (i.e., the definitions of security), computer scientists have developed common security mechanisms to protect computer systems. Early attempts of the protection mechanisms include authentication/identification, encryption, access control, etc. The goal of these mechanisms is to *prevent* unauthorized users from compromising the confidentiality, integrity as well as availability of the protected systems. Thus, they can be collectively called *prevention-based* techniques.

It has been noticed that the prevention-based techniques cannot assure the security of the systems being protected. For example, in 1988 the Internet worm brought down the majority of the Internet by taking advantage of the vulnerabilities in *rsh, fingerd,* and *sendmail* [Eichin and Rochis, 1989]. Even in year 2000, the so-called Distributed Denial of Service (DDoS) attacks [CERT, 1999a, CERT, 1999b] stopped several major commercial sites, including Yahoo and CNN, from functioning normally, though they were protected by prevention-based techniques such as firewalls. These incidents showed the inadequacy of the prevention-based techniques. Indeed, a deeper reason is that the processes with which human beings develop information systems are not error-proof: there may be bugs in the implementation of systems, and, moreover, there may be flaws in the design of information systems.

Intrusion detection was proposed to complement the prevention-based security measures [Anderson, 1980]. An intrusion is defined to be a violation of the security policy of the system [Kumar, 1995]; intrusion detection thus refers to the mechanisms that are developed to detect the violation of the system security policy. Intrusion detection is based on the assumption that intrusive activities are noticeably different from normal system activities and thus detectable [Denning, 1986]. Intrusion detection is not introduced to replace the prevention-based techniques such as authentication and access control; instead, it is intended to be used along with the existing security measures and detect the actions that (attempt to) bypass the security control of the system. Thus, intrusion detection is usually considered a second line of defense for computer and network systems.

Intrusion detection methods can be classified as *anomaly detection* or *misuse detection*. Anomaly detection is based on the normal behavior of a subject (e.g., a user, a host, or a network); any action that significantly deviates from the normal behavior is considered intrusive. For example, if a user usually compiles and debugs C programs during the working hours but never works at night, then an activity of editing the password file during the night is considered anomalous and may be an attack. Misuse detection looks for explicit patterns of known attacks. For example, to launch the password buffer overflow attack, the attacker needs to enter a password longer than the buffer allocated for the password so that he/she can override some memory locations (which are often in the stack). To detect such attacks, we can simply look at the length of the entered password. If it is longer than the buffer, then it is probably an attack. Real attacks are certainly more complex than this example; thus, more complicated techniques are required for misuse detection. Existing techniques for anomaly and misuse detection will be further discussed in Chapter 2.

2. Intrusion Detection in Distributed Systems

The rapid growth of the networks not only provides means for resource and information sharing, but also brings new challenges to intrusion detection. Due to the complexity and the amount of audit information generated by large-scale systems, traditional intrusion detection systems (IDSs), which were originally designed for individual hosts and small-scale networked systems, cannot be applied to large-scale systems directly.

However, it is necessary to perform intrusion detection in large-scale distributed systems in order to ensure the security of all (or most of) the component systems. The Internet Worm incident [Eichin and Rochis, 1989] and the Distributed Denial of Service (DDoS) attacks [CERT, 1999a, CERT, 1999b] have shown that attacks can really happen in a large scale and affect many computers connected to the network. In a distributed system, attacks usually involve more than one component system; it is difficult and sometimes impossible to decide whether some events in one place correspond to attacks without the information from other places.

It is usually beneficial to perform intrusion detection in a large scale. Sharing intrusion detection information among multiple systems can help improve their awareness of the situation, and thus help them detect or prevent intrusive activities. In particular, since attacks in distributed systems are usually launched or propagated from one computer system to another, detecting an attempt to attack in one system may help to prevent it from propagating to other systems. Moreover, having the overall picture of a distributed system gives the possibility to isolate the intrusive systems (e.g., the systems compromised by intruders) from the rest of the distributed systems.

Several approaches have been proposed to make IDSs scale up to large distributed systems. For example, EMERALD uses generic building blocks that can be deployed in a highly distributed manner. These building blocks can be organized in a hierarchical way, and the lower-level ones can send their analysis results to the higher-level one for further correlation. In addition, there has been efforts to enable different IDSs to share information among each other. For example, standards are being developed (e.g., IETF's Intrusion Detection Message Exchange Format (IDMEF) [Curry and Debar, 2001, Feinstein et al., 2001]) to make IDSs understand the information from other systems. (Chapter 2 will discuss related work on distributed intrusion detection in further details.)

This monograph presents a research effort in distributed intrusion detection performed by the authors. The starting point of this research is the observation that two intrinsic aspects of large distributed systems are often overlooked in previous approaches: (1) large distributed systems (e.g., the Internet) are usually heterogeneous, and (2) the components of a large system are often autonomous. Ignoring these aspects makes the IDSs rather restrictive and even unable to protect the systems as they are designed to. For example, an IDS specifically designed for UNIX systems may not understand the information provided by a Windows NT system, and thus cannot detect any intrusion on it. As another example, a distributed IDS may not be able to get some critical information from a system simply because the owner of the system does not want to provide it. A systematic way is needed to avoid the above situations and ensure the protection of large distributed and heterogeneous systems.

In addition, the previous approaches to sharing information among different IDSs is incomplete. All the previous work (e.g., CIDF, IETF's IDMEF [Curry and Debar, 2001] and the Hummer project [Frincke et al., 1998]) is to make

IDSs understand the information from other systems; little research is done to enable an IDS to request the information of interest from other places. The lack of such a capability may lead to inefficient communication between IDSs. If the sending IDSs send all the information to the receiving IDSs, the receiving ones may be overwhelmed by messages that they don't want. Not only the sending and the receiving IDSs have to process unnecessary messages, but network bandwidth is also wasted. On the other hand, if the sending IDSs do not send all the information, the receiving parties may miss some important messages. An easy way to deal with this problem is to simply classify or enumerate the possible requests for IDSs; however, this will require a lot of effort on classification or enumeration, and the resulting approach will be quite restrictive.

The goal of the work presented in this monograph is to study a systematic way to perform distributed intrusion detection in heterogeneous and autonomous systems. Specifically, we would like to develop a flexible way for IDSs to share information among each other and an efficient way to coordinate different IDSs to detect and correlate distributed attacks (events).

3. Summary of Contributions

The research contributions of this monograph consist of three complementary parts. The first contribution is an abstraction-based approach to addressing heterogeneity and autonomy of distributed systems. Specifically, the concept of system view is introduced to provide an abstract interface between different systems. On the one hand, system views hide the difference between heterogeneous systems; on the other hand, they describes what information an autonomous system is willing to provide to other systems.

The second contribution is a formal framework for modeling requests among cooperative IDSs and its application to Common Intrusion Detection Framework (CIDF). The first problem is how to enable an IDS to request specific information from another IDS. To address this problem, we propose to represent a request for an IDS as a pattern plus a transformation rule, where the pattern specifies the events that the requesting party is interested in and the transformation rule extracts interesting information from the events. The formal approach is also used to add a query facility to the Common Intrusion Detection Framework (CIDF). This method enables an IDS to form flexible requests for other systems.

The third contribution is a novel approach to representing distributed attacks and coordinating different IDSs for distributed event correlation. We first develop a hierarchical model aimed at supporting attack specification and event abstraction in distributed systems [Ning et al., 2001]. As distinguishing features, this model allows generic signatures that accommodate unknown variants of known attacks, and the event abstraction can be updated without changing either its specification or the attack signatures defined on the basis of the event abstraction. A decentralized method is then presented for autonomous but cooperative IDSs to perform the event correlation specified by signatures. Specifically, a signature is decomposed into finer units called *detection tasks*, each of which represents the activity to be monitored in one place. The IDSs (involved in a signature) then perform the detection tasks cooperatively according to the "dependency" relationships among these tasks. Our approach is superior to the existing centralized or hierarchical approaches in that (1) communication is more efficient by having different IDSs communicate with each other only when necessary, and (2) no centralized or hierarchical trust is required (trust is also decentralized in our approach). As an important application of distributed intrusion detection and event correlation, this approach can be used to represent and detect distributed (or coordinated) attacks that cannot be detected from a single place. An experimental system called CARDS has been implemented to test the feasibility of the proposed approaches.

4. Organization

The remainder of this monograph is organized as follows. The next chapter discusses the related work on intrusion detection. Chapter 3 presents the concept of system view, which is used as the interface between heterogeneous and autonomous systems. The notion of system view is the foundation of the abstraction-based approach. Chapter 4 describes the query model for representing requests for a certain IDS. Chapter 5 applies the formal model developed in 4 to add a query facility to Common Intrusion Specification Language (CISL), the language adopted by CIDF. Chapter 6 discusses the specification model that we use to represent the distributed event correlation (or distributed attacks in particular). Chapter 7 then presents the decentralized approach to coordinating different IDSs and detecting distributed attacks. Chapter 8 discusses a prototype system called *CARDS*, which was implemented to test the feasibility of our approach. Chapter 9 concludes this monograph. Appendices A and B give the Document Type Definitions (DTDs) used in CARDS as well as the XML representation of an example of distributed attacks and its detection tasks.

Chapter 2

AN OVERVIEW OF RELATED RESEARCH

Intrusions in an information system are the activities that violate the security policy of the system, and intrusion detection is the process to identify intrusions. Intrusion detection has been studied for over 20 years, since Anderson's report [Anderson, 1980]. It is based on the beliefs that an intruder's behavior will be noticeably different from that of a legitimate user and that many unauthorized actions will be detectable.

Intrusion detection methods can be classified as *anomaly detection* or *misuse detection*. Anomaly detection is based on the normal behavior of a subject (e.g., a user, a host, or a network); any action that significantly deviates from the normal behavior is considered intrusive. The normal behavior may be learned by observing the subject under normal operations, or specified based on prior knowledge. Numerous attempts have been made to build anomaly detection models, including statistical approaches [Anderson et al., 1995, Javits and Valdes, 1993, Smaha, 1988], machine learning and data mining approaches [Teng et al., 1990, Lane and Brodley, 1998, Fox et al., 1990, Ghosh et al., 1998, Barbará et al., 2001a, Barbará et al., 2001b], computer immunological approaches [Forrest et al., 1996, Forrest et al., 1994, Hofmeyr et al., 1998, Warrender et al., 1999, Sekar et al., 2001], specification-based approaches [Ko et al., 1997, Sekar et al., 2002], and static analysis [Wagner and Dean, 2001]. Moreover, several information-theoretic measures have been proposed to guide the construction of anomaly detection models [Lee. and Xiang, 2001].

Misuse detection represents intrusions in terms of the patterns of known attacks or system vulnerabilities; any action that conforms to the pattern of a known attack or vulnerability is considered intrusive. Several approaches have been proposed to represent known attacks or vulnerabilities, including rule-based languages [Lindqvist and Porras, 1999, Mounji, 1997, Mounji et al., 1995], STATL [Eckmann et al., 2002], CPA [Kumar, 1995, Kumar and Spafford, 1994], LAMBDA [Cuppens and Ortalo, 2000], and MuSig [Lin et al., 1998, Ning et al., 2001]. The general philosophy of these approaches is to make the representation mechanisms easy to use and yet capable of representing most (if not all) known attacks. Constructing a correct signature for known attacks, however, is a time-consuming and non-trivial task. A data mining framework has been developed to automatically generate misuse detection models from historical data [Lee and Stolfo, 1998, Lee et al., 1998, Lee et al., 1999, Lee and Stolfo, 2000].

Many commercial and research IDSs have been developed using anomaly and/or misuse detection techniques. These systems are generally classified as host-based IDSs, network-based IDSs, or distributed IDSs. Host-based IDSs detect attacks using information from individual hosts, such as host audit trails or shell command history [Ilgun et al., 1995, Kummar and Spafford, 1995, Lin et al., 1998]; network-based IDSs perform detection by analyzing network traffic [Roesch, 1999, Vigna and Kemmerer, 1999, Vigna and Kermmerer, 1998, Ranum et al., 1997, Chang et al., 2001, Jou et al., 2000]; distributed IDSs analyze information from multiple sources, including individual hosts and network traffic, and typically distribute the workload over multiple systems [Vigna and Kermmerer, 2001, Porras and Neumann, 1997, Mounji, 1997, Mounji et al., 1995, Snapp et al., 1991, Spafford and Zamboni, 2000, Ning et al., 2001, Ning et al., 2002].

Our work falls into the research domain of detecting intrusions distributed over multiple systems, including distributed intrusion detection systems and other related techniques. Early distributed intrusion detection systems collect audit data from distributed component systems but analyze them in a central place (e.g., DIDS [Snapp et al., 1991], ISM [Heberlein et al., 1992], NADIR [Hochberg et al., 1993], NSTAT [Kemmerer, 1997] and ASAX [Mounji, 1997, Mounji et al., 1995]). Although audit data are usually reduced before being sent to the central analysis unit, the scalability of such systems is limited due to the centralized analysis.

Recent systems paid more attention to the scalability issue (e.g., EMERALD [Porras and Neumann, 1997], GrIDS [Staniford-Chen et al., 1996], AAFID [Spafford and Zamboni, 2000], and CSM [White et al., 1996]). EMERALD adopts a recursive framework in which generic building blocks can be deployed in a highly distributed manner [Porras and Neumann, 1997]. Both misuse detection and statistical anomaly detection are used in EMERALD. GrIDS aims at large distributed systems and performs intrusion detection by aggregating computer and network information into activity graphs which reveal the causal structure of network activity [Staniford-Chen et al., 1996]. AAFID is a distributed intrusion detection platform, which consists of four types of components: agents, filters, transceivers and monitors [Spafford and Zamboni, 2000]. These components can be organized in a tree structure, where child and parent components communicate with each other. AAFID emphasizes on the architecture aspect of distributed intrusion detection; detailed mechanism for performing distributed intrusion detection is not addressed. JiNao is an IDS that detects intrusions against network routing protocols [Chang et al., 2001, Jou et al., 2000, Wu et al., 2000]. The current implementation of JiNao focuses on the OSPF (Open Shortest Path First) routing protocol. A distinguished feature of JiNao is that it can be integrated into existing network management systems. It is mentioned that JiNao can be used for distributed intrusion detection [Jou et al., 2000, Wu et al., 2000]; however, no specific mechanisms have been provided for doing so.

In terms of the way of performing distributed intrusion detection, our approach differs from these systems as follows: While our approach decomposes and coordinates distributed event collection and analysis according to the intrinsic relationships between the distributed events, the aforementioned systems either have no specific way to coordinate different IDSs (e.g., JiNao [Jou et al., 2000, Wu et al., 2000]), or rely on some predefined hierarchical organization, which is usually determined by administrative concerns (e.g., EMERALD [Porras and Neumann, 1997], GrIDS [Staniford-Chen et al., 1996]). Compared with the hierarchical approach, our approach has the advantage that the component IDSs can exchange necessary information without forwarding it along the hierarchy.

NetSTAT is an application of STAT [Ilgun et al., 1995] to network-based intrusion detection [Vigna and Kemmerer, 1999, Vigna and Kermmerer, 1998]. Based on the attack scenarios and the network fact modeled as a hyper-graph, NetSTAT automatically chooses places to probe network activities and applies the state transition analysis. Our approach is similar to NetSTAT in the sense that both approaches can decide what information needs to be collected in various places. However, our approach also differs from NetSTAT in the following ways. NetSTAT is specific to network-based intrusion detection, while our approach is generic to any kind of distributed intrusion detection. Moreover, NetSTAT collects the network events in a distributed way, but analyzes them in a central place. In contrast, our approach analyzes the distributed events in a decentralized way, that is, the events are analyzed as being collected in various places.

Event abstraction has long been recognized as an important issue in intrusion detection as well as many other areas. It not only removes the irrelevant details, but also hides the difference between heterogeneous systems. Several systems have adopted components for event abstraction. ARMD explicitly brought up the concept of abstract system to provide the abstract representation of system information [Lin, 1998, Lin et al., 1998]. AAFID introduces filters as a data abstraction layer for intrusion detection agents [Spafford and Zamboni, 2000]. JiNao adopts an event abstraction module to transform low-level network activities into high-level events [Jou et al., 2000, Wu et al., 2000]. (There are other examples; however, we do not enumerate them here.) Our approach further extends these ideas by providing a hierarchical framework for event abstraction. In particular, we view event abstraction as a dynamic process (instead of a preparation stage as in most of the previous approaches). The advantage is that we can update the semantics of event abstraction without changing either its specification or the signatures defined on the basis of it, and thus have generic signatures that can accommodate the variants of known attacks.

Several approaches have been proposed to represent known attacks. Among them are the rule-based languages such as P-BEST [Lindqvist and Porras, 1999] and RUSSEL [Mounji, 1997, Mounji et al., 1995], the state transition analysis toolkit (STAT) [Ilgun, 1993, Ilgun et al., 1995] and its extension POSTAT [Ho et al., 1998], the Colored PetriNet Automaton (CPA) [Kumar, 1995, Kumar and Spafford, 1994], and JiNao Finite State Machine (JFSM) [Jou et al., 2000, Wu et al., 2000]. The general philosophy of these approaches is to make the representation mechanisms easy to use and yet capable of representing most of the known attacks (if not all). Our representation mechanism can be considered as a variation of STAT or CPA, which removes the explicit states from the attack patterns. A new feature of our method is that it allows events to be extracted from signatures so that attack (or event) patterns can be specified in a hierarchical way. Moreover, our representation mechanism gives an opportunity to decompose a distributed attack pattern into smaller units that can be executed in a distributed manner.

Common Intrusion Detection Framework (CIDF) is an effort that is aimed at enabling different intrusion detection and response (IDR) components to interoperate and share information and resources [Kahn et al., 1998b, Porras et al., 1998]. CIDF views IDR systems as composed of four kinds components that communicate via message passing: Event Generators (E-boxes), Event Analyzers (A-boxes), Event Databases (D-boxes) and Response Units (R-boxes). A communication framework and a common intrusion specification language are provided to assist the interoperation among CIDF components [Feiertag et al., 2000a, Kahn et al., 1998a]. Several efforts have tried to improve CIDF components' ability to interoperate with each other: The Intrusion Detection Inter-component Adaptive Negotiation (IDIAN) protocol helps cooperating CIDF components to reach an agreement on each other's capabilities and needs [Feiertag et al., 2000b]; MADAM ID uses CIDF to automatically get audit data, build models, and distribute signatures for novel attacks so that the gap between the discovery and the detection of new attacks can be reduced [Lee et al., 2000, Lee and Stolfo, 2000]; finally, the query facility for CIDF reported in this monograph enables CIDF components to request specific information from each other.

IETF's Intrusion Detection Working Group (IDWG) has been working on data formats and exchange procedures for sharing information among IDSs, response systems, and management systems. XML has been chosen to provide the common format, and an Intrusion Detection Message Exchange Format (IDMEF) has been defined in an Internet draft [Curry and Debar, 2001]. IDWG uses the Blocks Extensible Exchange Protocol (BEEP) as the application protocol framework for exchanging intrusion detection messages between different systems [Rose, 2001]; an Intrusion Detection Exchange Protocol (IDXP) is specified as a BEEP profile [Feinstein et al., 2001], and a Tunnel profile is provided for different systems to exchange messages through firewalls [New, 2001].

We view CIDF, IDMEF (IDXP) and their extensions as complementary to ours. First, in terms of representation, CIDF, IDMEF (IDXP), and their extensions provide common message formats and exchange procedures for IDSs to interoperate and understand each other, while our work provides a framework for event abstraction as well as specification of queries and known intrusion patterns. Second, neither CIDF nor IDWG provides any specific way to coordinate different IDSs (indeed, as standards, they try to avoid any specific mechanism). Though MADAM ID enables different IDSs to collaborate with each other, the collaboration is limited to collecting audit data for new attacks and distributing newly discovered signatures [Lee et al., 2000]. In contrast, our approach decomposes a signature for a distributed attack into smaller units, distributes these units to different IDSs, and coordinates these IDSs to detect the attack.

The Hummer project is intended to share information among different IDSs [Frincke et al., 1998]. In particular, the relationships between different IDSs (e.g., peer, friend, manager/subordinate relationships) and policy issues (e.g., access control policy, cooperation policy) are studied, and a prototype system HummingBird was developed to address these issues. However, the Hummer project is to address the general data sharing issue; what information needs to be shared and how the information is used are out of its scope. In contrast, our decentralized detection approach addresses the issue of efficiently detecting specific attacks; it is able to specify what information is needed from each site and how the information is analyzed. Indeed, our decentralized detection approach can be combined with the Hummer system to fully take advantage of its data collection capability.

Our work is based on a host-based misuse detection system named ARMD [Lin, 1998, Lin et al., 1998]. The work in this monograph further extends the result in ARMD in several ways. First, the attack specification model is extended to allow the representation of attacks across multiple systems. In particular, our model assumes interval-based events rather than point-based events; thus, not only event records directly derived from audit trails but also compound events are accommodated. Moreover, the revised model adopts the notion of negative event and can take into account exceptional situations. Second, the revised model allows hierarchical specification of event patterns, which not only provides a way to model distributed attacks, but also a framework for automatic event abstraction. Finally, we develop a decentralized approach to detecting distributed attacks.

Chapter 3

SYSTEM VIEW AND EVENT HISTORY

In this chapter, we propose to use an intermediate layer, which we call *system view*, to provide a unified representation of the information provided by different types of systems.

A system view serves two purposes. First, it can hide the differences between heterogeneous systems. For example, most of the platforms (e.g., UNIX and Windows NT) have login process to authenticate users. Though the status of the login processes on different platforms may be recorded in different formats (e.g., BSM on Solaris and Windows Event Logger on Windows), we can transform such information into a unified representation on a common system view that abstracts the common features of login processes. Certainly, the correspondence between the same kind of information on different platforms may be more complex than simple one-to-one mappings between audit records. However, compared with the possible attacks that we may discover and describe, the correspondence between the information on different platforms is relatively static, and it is fairly easy to write simple programs to transform information on heterogeneous platforms to a unified representation.

Second, a system view can hide the detailed information provided by an autonomous system. As we discussed earlier, an autonomous system that is willing to collaborate with other systems may have its own concerns about the privacy and confidentiality of its local information. It may want to provide information to a certain degree instead of giving out all kinds of information. System view then serves as an interface that specifies what kind of information is exported from the autonomous system. The information on the autonomous system may be cleansed and/or aggregated before being provided through the system view.

In the remainder of this chapter, we clarify how we formalize the concept of system view.

1.   System View and Event History

Intuitively, a system view provides an abstract representation of a system. The system underlying a system view may be one single host, a network segment, or a distributed system consisting of several hosts.

Both event information and relationships among system entities are provided through a system view. Events represent what have happened or are happening in the system, while relationships among system entities represent the system state at certain times. For instance, the fact that two files are owned by the same user can be represented by a relationship *same_owner* between them.

The time when an event occurs is intrinsic to the event. In distributed environments, the intrusion detection related events are usually not instantaneous in terms of time. (For example, a TCP connection could span several hours.) To accommodate such events, we consider that each event has a duration and associate an interval-based timestamp with it. Notation-wise, each timestamp is denoted in the form of [*begin_time*, *end_time*], representing the starting and the ending points of the time interval, respectively.

We use a predicate to represent a relationship among system entities. A predicate for a particular relationship takes the entities as arguments, and returns True if the relationship is satisfied, and False otherwise. For example, the predicate *same_owner(var_file_x, var_file_y)* determines whether the owners of *var_file_x* and *var_file_y* are the same user. It returns True if a single user owns both files, and False otherwise.

The relationships among system entities may be dynamic, i.e., the relationships may change over time. For example, suppose a user is the owner of both files *file_x* and *file_y* at a certain time, but later the superuser changes the owner of *file_x* to another user. Then *same_owner(file_x, file_y)* returns True before the change of owner, while returns False afterwards. Thus, notation-wise, we insert symbols "[*var_time*]" between the predicate name and its arguments, indicating that time is one necessary argument of the predicate. We call such predicates *dynamic predicates*. Hence the dynamic predicate for determining file owners can be denoted *same_owner[var_time](var_file_x, var_file_y)*, which becomes a regular predicate when "*var_time*" is replaced with a constant time point. For example, *same_owner[t](file_x, file_y)* is True if and only if the owners of *file_x* and *file_y* are the same at time *t*. Note that "static", or regular predicates are special cases of dynamic predicates.

The notion of system view is formally stated as follows.

DEFINITION 3.1 A *system view* is a pair $(EvtSch, PredSet)$, where $EvtSch$ (called *event schema*) is a set of event attribute names, each with an associated domain of values, and $PredSet$ is a set of dynamic predicate names. An *event* e on $(EvtSch, PredSet)$ is a tuple on $EvtSch$ with a timestamp [$begin\_time$, end_time].

A system view serves as an interface of the information of interest. Though a system view itself is fixed once defined, the information provided through it can be extended. For example, when we define a system view for TCP/IP based denial of service (DOS) attacks, we may abstract the system view from *Teardrop* and *Land* attacks (Please refer to [Kendall, 1999] for the details of the attacks). However, we may later discover *SYN flooding* and *Ping Of Death* attacks, which are also TCP/IP based DOS attacks. Such newly discovered information can be directly provided through the existing system view without changing either the system view specification or the signatures already defined on the basis of its instances.

The timestamp variables *begin_time* and *end_time* are implicit attributes of the event schema, which collectively represent the timestamps of events on the system view. The information provided through a system view, including both event and state information, is formalized as an event history on the corresponding system view.

DEFINITION 3.2 An *event history* on the system view $(EvtSch, PredSet)$ consists of (1) a finite set of events $\{e_1, \ldots, e_m\}$ on $(EvtSch, PredSet)$ and (2) an instantiation of the dynamic predicate names in $PredSet$ such that for each p in $PredSet$ and each time point t when an event occurs, p is instantiated as a regular predicate, denoted $p[t](x_1, \ldots, x_k)$ (i.e., for each instantiation of $x_1, \ldots, x_k$, $p[t](x_1, \ldots, x_k)$ gives True or False).

In a system view, the event attribute names provide a relation schema for the events, and the dynamic predicates represent the relationships among system entities. The events that occur in the underlying system are described as timestamped tuples on the event schema. At a particular time t, a dynamic predicate becomes a regular predicate, representing a relationship of the system entities at time t.

EXAMPLE 3.1 To report DOS attacks that disable one or all the TCP ports of a host, a network monitor may have a system view *TCPDOSAttacks* = $(EvtSch1, \emptyset)$, where $EvtSch1 = \{VictimIP, VictimPort\}$. Each DOS attack is reported as an event on $(EvtSch1, \emptyset)$. The domain of *VictimIP* is the set of IP addresses, and the domain of *VictimPort* is the set of all TCP ports plus -1. *VictimPort* being -1 means that all TCP ports (of the host) are disabled. An event history on *TCPDOSAttacks* is shown in table 3.1.

Table 3.1. An event history on the system view *TCPDOSAttacks*

event	VictimIP	VictimPort	begin_time	end_time
e_1	10.0.0.1	80	19:37:01	19:43:05
e_2	10.0.0.2	23	19:38:15	19:38:15
e_3	10.0.0.255	−1	19:40:50	19:45:00
e_4	10.0.0.3	−1	19:44:15	19:44:15
...	...	...	...	...

As another example, a host may have a system view *LocalTCPConn* = (*EvtSch2, PredSet2*) for the TCP connections observed on the local host, where the event schema *EvtSch2* = {*SrcIP, SrcPort, DstIP, DstPort*} and the set of dynamic predicates *PredSet2* = {*LocalIP[t](var_IP), Trust[t](var_host)*}. The domains of the attributes are clear from the names. The dynamic predicate *LocalIP[t](var_IP)* evaluates to True if and only if *var_IP* is an IP address belonging to the local host at time *t*, and the dynamic predicate *Trust[t](var_host)* evaluates to True if and only if *var_host* is trusted by the local host at time *t*. Examples of the event histories on *LocalTCPConn* are omitted.

A system view may also be provided by an IDS. A system view of an IDS represents the interface through which the IDS provides attack related information. The attacks that the IDS detects or the event information that the IDS is unable to process can be provided as events on the system view, and the state of the IDS or the system monitored by the IDS can be provided as dynamic predicates. The following example shows a system view provided by a host-based IDS.

EXAMPLE 3.2 The system view provided by a host-based IDS can be ({*action, user, file_name*}, {*same_obj[−](x_1, x_2)*}). The domain of *action* is {*login, logout, read, write, exec*}, the domains for *user* and *file_name* are the strings. The dynamic predicate name *same_obj[−](x_1, x_2)* determines whether x_1 and x_2 refer to the same file object at a certain time. Some possible events on the system view are shown in table 3.2. For each event, the dynamic predicate *same_obj* is instantiated to a boolean function that takes two file names as arguments and returns True or False as output. For example, if the file */tmp/myfile* has a link to */etc/dfs/dfstab* at the time when event e_{i+4} occurs, then *same_obj[e_{i+4}](/tmp/myfile, /etc/dfs/dfstab)* returns True. Timestamps are omitted from table 3.2.

One system can provide a number of different views. These views may represent different aspects of the system. For example, an IDS can provide one system view for the execution of shell commands by users, and another view

Table 3.2. An event history provided by a host-based IDS

event	action	user	file_name
...	...	...	...
e_i	*login*	*Bob*	—
e_{i+1}	*write*	*Joe*	*/etc/dfs/dfstab*
e_{i+2}	*read*	*Tom*	*/home/tom/paper.tex*
e_{i+3}	*logout*	*Joe*	—
e_{i+4}	*read*	*Bob*	*/tmp/myfile*
...	...	...	...

for forwarded IP packets. An IDS can also provide, for the same aspect of the underlying system, different information via different views. As an example, to an administrative partner within its organization, an IDS may provide a view with very detailed information (e.g., all the security relevant events), but to a party in another organization, it may present a view with very concise information (e.g., alerts of attacks).

1.1 Qualitative Temporal Relationships between Events

The representation and reasoning about the qualitative temporal relationships between interval-based events have been extensively studied by the AI community [Allen, 1983, Freksa, 1992]. With these relationships, we can provide a more concise representation of the patterns among events.

Here we quote the thirteen relationships between intervals [Allen, 1983] and the eleven relationships between semi-intervals [Freksa, 1992] as the qualitative relationships between events. Table 3.3 shows the relationships between two interval-based events e_1 and e_2. The inverse relation in the table refers to the relation derived by switching the positions of the events in the original relation. For example, the inverse relation of e_1 before e_2 is e_1 after e_2, which is equivalent to e_2 before e_1.

Complex qualitative (temporal) relationships between two events can be represented by logical combinations of the aforementioned relations. For example, the constraint that events e_1 and e_2 do not overlap in time can be represented by

$$(e_1 \text{ before } e_2) \text{ or } (e_1 \text{ after } e_2),$$

or simply e_1(before or after)e_2. In the following, we will take advantage of these qualitative temporal relationships to describe attack signatures.

Table 3.3. The qualitative temporal relationships between two events

relation	meaning	inverse relation
e_1 equal e_2	$e_1.begin\_time = e_2.begin\_time$ and $e_1.end\_time = e_2.end\_time$	equal
e_1 before e_2	$e_1.end\_time < e_2.begin\_time$	after
e_1 meets e_2	$e_1.end\_time = e_2.begin\_time$	inv-meets
e_1 overlaps e_2	$e_1.begin\_time < e_2.begin\_time$ and $e_1.end\_time < e_2.end\_time$ and $e_1.end\_time > e_2.begin\_time$	inv-overlaps
e_1 during e_2	$e_1.begin\_time > e_2.begin\_time$ and $e_1.end\_time < e_2.end\_time$	inv-during
e_1 starts e_2	$e_1.begin\_time = e_2.begin\_time$ and $e_1.end\_time < e_2.end\_time$	inv-starts
e_1 finishes e_2	$e_1.begin\_time > e_2.begin\_time$ and $e_1.end\_time = e_2.end\_time$	inv-finishes
e_1 older (than) e_2	$e_1.begin\_time < e_2.begin\_time$	younger (than)
e_1 head-to-head e_2	$e_1.begin\_time = e_2.begin\_time$	head-to-head
e_1 survives e_2	$e_1.end\_time < e_2.end\_time$	survived-by
e_1 tail-to-tail e_2	$e_1.end\_time > e_2.end\_time$	tail-to-tail
e_1 precedes e_2	$e_1.end\_time <= e_2.begin\_time$	succeeds
e_1 contemporary e_2	$e_1.begin\_time < e_2.end\_time$ and $e_2.begin\_time < e_1.end\_time$	contemporary
e_1 born-before-death e_2	$e_1.begin\_time < e_2.end\_time$	die-after-birth

Chapter 4

MODELING REQUEST AMONG COOPERATING INTRUSION DETECTION SYSTEMS

In this chapter, we propose a formal model to represent the requests among autonomous but cooperative IDSs on the basis of system views. With a system view stating the schema of the information provided by an IDS, a request (which we call a *query*) for the information from the IDS is formulated as *a pattern plus a transformation rule*. A query consists of both a set of of conditions and a transformation rule. The conditions tell what events are related to the request, and the transformation rule extracts useful information into the right form from the related events. Not only requests about single events but also those regarding the interrelationship among multiple events are considered in this formalization.

In contrast to a signature-based intrusion detection model that cares more about the existence of events that match attack signatures, our model is more concerned with flexible manipulation of the information associated with the events that match a request. The advantage of our approach is that not only it permits flexible specification of requests, but it may also be possible to reuse existing intrusion detection software modules and signatures.

Note that our approach is independent of the message transmission model, which can be either a push or a pull model. Indeed, this approach not only enables an IDS to send queries to other systems, but also allows it to set up traps at remote systems.

In order to scale our approach to a large, heterogeneous network, we propose to specify queries on the expectations of system views instead of those provided by IDSs. In some cases, the resulting mismatch between queries and the system views provided by IDSs can be resolved automatically by the system through the built-in expert knowledge.

The rest of the chapter is organized as follows. Section 4.1 describes our model for the specification of queries. Section 4.2 discusses the approaches to scaling the model to large, heterogeneous environments. Section 4.3 compares our approach with some alternative approaches and discusses the relationship with signature-based intrusion detection as well as some implementation issues.

1. Query

Queries are used on system views to retrieve information. A query is a combination of a set of constraints that the relevant events must satisfy, and a transformation rule (more precisely, a SQL statement) to derive the requested information from these relevant events.

There are three kinds of constraints: (1) the qualitative temporal relationship between the events, (2) the conditions that a single event must satisfy (single-event condition), and (3) the conditions that multiple events must satisfy (multiple-event condition).

We use directed graph with labeled arc to denote the qualitative temporal relationships that the events must have. Each node in the directed graph represents an event, and each labeled arc from one node to another indicates that the events involved in the arc must satisfy the qualitative temporal relationship specified by the label. For example, if an arc from node n_1 to n_2 is labeled *before*, then the event represented by n_1 must occur before the occurrence of the event represented by n_2.

We use single-event conditions to specify the events that can be associated with a node. Selected event attribute values are then assigned to variables if the single-event condition is satisfied by an event. We use multiple-event conditions on the variables assigned in multiple nodes to specify the combination of events that can be associated with the nodes of labeled directed graph. Since some relationships (i.e., those represented by dynamic predicates) change over time, we allow a multiple-event condition to be specified for each node, meaning that the multiple-event condition should be satisfied at the time when the event associated with the node occurs.

For each combination of events that satisfies the above conditions, the variables contain the requested information derived from these events. We can think of the variable names as providing a relation schema. A tuple in this relation corresponds to the values in the variables from one combination of events that satisfies the conditions, and the relation consists of all such tuples. A SQL statement is used to specify the transformation that derives information from this relation into a desired form (e.g., count the number of tuples).

The single-event condition and the multiple-event condition are formalized as follows.

DEFINITION 4.1 Given a system view (R, C), a *single-event condition on* (R, C) is a Boolean formula with atoms being either (1) comparisons between event attribute names in R and constants, or (2) of the form $c[-](a_1, \ldots, a_k)$, where c is a dynamic predicate name in C and $a_1, \ldots, a_k$ are event attribute names in R or constants. A single-event condition is denoted by $p(-)$ which evaluates to True or False when "$-$" is replaced with an event e (i.e., the event attribute names in the Boolean formula are replaced with the corresponding values from the event, and each dynamic predicate $c[-](a_1, \ldots, a_k)$ is replaced with $c[e](a_1, \ldots, a_k)$).

DEFINITION 4.2 Given a system view (R, C), a *multiple-event condition on* (R, C) *with k variables* is a Boolean formula with atoms being either (1) comparisons between variables and constants, or (2) of the form $c[-](u_1, \ldots, u_l)$, where c is a dynamic predicate name in C and $u_1, \ldots, u_l$ are variables or constants. A multiple-event condition is denoted by $g(x_1, \ldots, x_k, -)$ which evaluates to True or False when each x_i is replaced with a constant and the last place $(-)$ with an event.

A single-event condition involves event attribute names and constants, while a multiple-event condition involves variables, which can be assigned attribute values from multiple events, and constants.

EXAMPLE 4.1 Consider the system view in example 3.2. We can have the following single-event conditions on this view: $p_1(-)$: $action = read$, and $p_2(-)$: $action = write$. (Note that neither condition involves dynamic predicates.) The third and the last event shown in table 3.2 satisfy $p_1(-)$, while the second event satisfies $p_2(-)$. Let var_file1 and var_file2 be two variables representing file names. Then $g(var\_file1, var\_file2, -)$: $same\_object[-](var\_file1, var\_file2)$ is a multiple-event condition that determines whether two file names refer to the same file.

We are now ready to formally define the notion of a query.

DEFINITION 4.3 Given a system view (R, C), a *query* on the view is a 8-tuple $\mathcal{Q} = (N, E, L, V, P, A, G, S)$, where

- (N, E) is a connected directed graph,

- L is a mapping that maps each arch in E to a qualitative temporal relationship between two events,

- V is a finite set of variables such that all variables appear in the assignments in A,

- P is a mapping that maps each node in N to a single-event condition on (R, C),

- A is a mapping that maps each node in N to a set of assignments of event attributes to variables (denoted as, e.g., $x := attribute\_name$) such that all variables are in V and no single variable appear in more than one assignment,

- G is a mapping that maps each node in N to a multiple-event condition on (R, C) whose variables are all in V, and

- S is a SQL query [Date and Darwen, 1997] on a relation whose attributes are exactly the variables in V. This relation is denoted as (V).

To have a better illustration, we represent a query as a labeled graph. For each query $Q = (N, E, L, V, P, A, G, S)$, the components N, E and L are represented by a labeled directed graph, the components P, A and G are represented by the single-event conditions, assignments and multiple-event conditions associated with each node, the set of variables V is implicitly represented by all the variables appearing in the assignments, and the component S is represented by the transformation rule associated with the whole graph.

The following examples show some queries that may be posed by cooperating IDSs.

EXAMPLE 4.2 This example shows a query that may be sent by an IDS to trace a suspicious user. Tracing techniques have been studied by various research groups and some solutions specialized for this problem have been proposed (e.g., thumbprinting [Staniford-Chen and Heberlein, 1995]). Here we show how we can achieve the same purpose through the cooperation of IDSs.

Suppose the IDS monitoring host A detects a suspicious user who remotely logged in from host B, and wants to trace the origin of this user. The IDS for host A discovers that this user is connected through a TCP connection from host B port PB to host A port PA at time tm'. It starts the tracing by posing the query Q shown in figure 4.1 to the IDS for host B.

The system view underlying this query is (R, C), where the event schema R is {$login\_session$, $event$, $user$, src_host, src_port, dst_host, dst_port, $duration$} and the dynamic predicate set C is {$start\_within(s_1, s_2)$}. The meaning of the event attributes are clear from their names. (Note that src and dst are abbreviations for $source$ and $destination$.) The dynamic predicate $start\_within(s_1, s_2)$ is to determine whether login_session s_2 is started (directly or indirectly) from within login_session s_1.

Informally, this query is to ask: From where and when did the suspicious user log into host B, given the clue that he (or she) maintained a TCP connection from host B port PB to host A port PA at time tm? Node $n1$ stands for a login event, and node $n2$ for the TCP connection through which the suspicious user remotely logged into host A. The multiple-event condition $g2$ selects all the login events that are (directly or indirectly) in the same login session as the

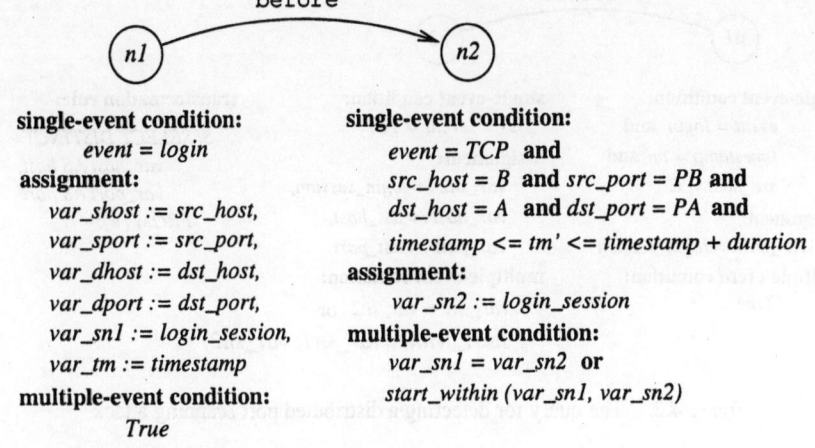

single-event condition:
 event = login
assignment:
 var_shost := src_host,
 var_sport := src_port,
 var_dhost := dst_host,
 var_dport := dst_port,
 var_sn1 := login_session,
 var_tm := timestamp
multiple-event condition:
 True

single-event condition:
 event = TCP and
 src_host = B and *src_port = PB* and
 dst_host = A and *dst_port = PA* and
 timestamp <= tm' <= timestamp + duration
assignment:
 var_sn2 := login_session
multiple-event condition:
 var_sn1 = var_sn2 or
 start_within (var_sn1, var_sn2)

transformation rule:

 SELECT var_shost AS src_host, var_sport AS src_port,
    var_dhost AS dst_host, var_dport AS dst_port,
    var_tm AS timestamp
 FROM (V)
 WHERE var_tm <= ALL (SELECT var_tm FROM (V));

Figure 4.1. The query for tracing suspicious users

TCP connection. Finally, the SQL statement S retrieves the host information of the earliest among these login events. This must be the host from which the suspicious user logged into B. If the *src_host* in the answer of S is B, the IDS for host A can then determine B is the origin of the suspicious user. Otherwise, suppose the answer to the query is ($src\_host = C, src\_port = PC, dst\_host = B, dst\_port = PB', timestamp = tm$), then the IDS for host A will send host C a similar query with the new information to determine the origin of the user. This process may continue until the origin of the user is found.

Another alternative is to send with the query a tracing directive, which tells the IDS being queried that after getting the query result, it should instantiate another tracing query and continue the process until the origin of the user is found. An IDS may also save a tracing query along with the query result. When an IDS instantiates a tracing query that is the same as a previously saved one, it may use the saved query result instead of resending the query. This approach can potentially improve the performance when a number of hosts want to trace the same user.

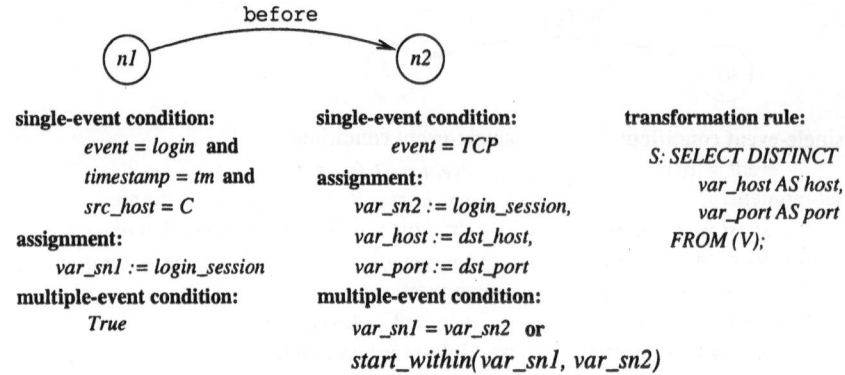

before

Figure 4.2. The query for detecting a distributed port scanning attack

EXAMPLE 4.3 In the previous example, suppose the IDS for host A suspects that the suspicious user attempted to distribute a TCP port scanning (e.g., with NMAP) over host A and B (and even more hosts) to avoid being detected. The IDS for A may ask the IDS for B the distinct hosts and ports that the suspicious user has connected to from host B by sending the query shown in figure 4.2. It can then combine the information from both host A and B to determine whether there is a distributed port scanning or not. Here we assume that the IDS for A has known that the suspicious user logged into B from host C at time tm from the answer to the previous query in example 4.2. We also assume that no two events on a single host have the same timestamp.

This query is to ask: list the distinct destination hosts and ports that the the suspicious user have connected to after login. Node $n1$ stands for the event that the user logged in, and node $n2$ for a TCP connection event. The multiple-event condition associated with node $n2$ selects all TCP connection events that are (directly or indirectly) in the same login session as the login event. The assignment associated with node $n2$ then get the destination host and port of the relevant TCP connections and the SQL statement generates the result by removing duplicate tuples.

1.1 Query Result

The *result* to a query is the information that is retrieved through the system view according to the query. We now formally discuss the result of a query on an event history.

DEFINITION 4.4 Let $\mathcal{H}$ be an event history on the system view (R, C), and $Q = (N, E, L, V, P, A, G, S)$ a query on (R, C). We say the events $e_1, \ldots, e_m$ in $\mathcal{H}$ *match* the query Q if there exists a one-to-one mapping $\pi : N \to \{e_1, \ldots, e_m\}$ such that

- for each arc (n_1, n_2) in E such that (n_1, n_2) is mapped to a qualitative temporal relationship $\cdot R\cdot$, if $\pi(n_1) = e_i$ and $\pi(n_2) = e_j$ (i.e., e_i and e_j are assigned to n_1 and n_2 respectively), then $e_i \cdot R\cdot e_j$,

- for each node n in N with single-event condition $p_n(-)$ and assignment a_n, if $\pi(n) = e_i$, then $p_n(e_i) = True$, and the variables in a_n are assigned with the corresponding attribute values,

- for each node n in N with multiple-event condition $g_n(x_1, \ldots, x_k, -)$, if $\pi(n) = e_i$, then $g_n(x_1, \ldots, x_k, e_i) = True$ with $x_1, \ldots, x_k$ replaced with the values assigned in (2).

The events $e_1, \ldots, e_m$ above are collectively called a *match* between the history $\mathcal{H}$ and the query $\mathcal{Q}$.

The set of events that matches a query are the events containing the requested information. When a set of events matches a query, each event is assigned to a node in the query, and the conditions specified in the query, i.e., the temporal order between events, the single-event condition, and the multiple-event condition, are all satisfied by these events.

DEFINITION 4.5 Let $\mathcal{H}$ be an event history on the system view (R, C), and $\mathcal{Q}$ a query on (R, C). The *intermediate result* of $\mathcal{Q}$ on the history $\mathcal{H}$ is the relation whose schema consists of the variables in V, and each tuple in the relation consists of the values assigned to the variables in a match between events in $\mathcal{H}$ and $\mathcal{Q}$. The *final result* of $\mathcal{Q}$ on the history $\mathcal{H}$ is the resulting relation of executing the SQL query S on the intermediate result.

EXAMPLE 4.4 Suppose host B in example 4.2 has the events shown in table 4.1, and the time when the suspicious user is discovered to have the TCP connection is $tm = 8$. (To make the table fit in the page, we abbreviate the attribute names *login_session, duration* and *timestamp* as *LS, DUR* and *TS*, respectively.) The last event shown in table 4.1 corresponds to this TCP connection. Suppose it is user *Bob* who logged into B as user *El* at time 5, then *start_within*$(1, 2)$ returns True after time 5. Therefore, we have the intermediate result shown in table 4.2. The final result gives host C after executing the SQL statement since C is the source host of the earliest login event.

EXAMPLE 4.5 According to the previous query result of example 4.3, the suspicious user logged into B from C at time 1. So the IDS for host A will use $host = C$ and $tm = 1$ in the query shown in figure 4.2. The intermediate result and the final result is shown in table 4.3, which says that the user made TCP connections to two distinct ports after login.

Table 4.1. Events on host *B*

LS	event	user	src_host	src_port	dst_host	dst_port	DUR	TS
1	login	Bob	C	PC	B	PB2	-	1
1	TCP	Bob	B	PB3	D	PD	20	3
2	login	El	B	-	B	-	-	5
2	TCP	El	B	PB	A	PA	25	6

Table 4.2. Result of the query shown in figure 4.1

Intermediate result

var_shost	var_sport	var_dhost	var_dport	var_sn1	var_sn2	var_tm
C	PC	B	PB2	1	2	1
B	-	B	-	2	2	5

Final result

src_host	src_port	dst_host	dst_port	timestamp
C	PC	B	PB2	1

Table 4.3. Result of the query shown in figure 4.2

Intermediate result

var_sn1	var_sn2	var_host	var_port
1	1	D	PD
1	2	A	PA

Final result

host	port
D	PD
A	PA

2. Scaling to Large and Heterogeneous Environments

In this section, we attempts to scale our approach to large, heterogeneous environments. We first introduce the notions of expected view and provided view to make query specification scalable, then study the resolution of the resulting mismatch between a query and an IDS.

2.1 Expected View and Provided View

As mentioned earlier, a system view of an IDS is an interface used by other systems to retrieve information. In a large network, there are potentially many different system views. Indeed, there are different IDSs that belong to different organizations. Also, different systems monitored by IDSs can have different features. For example, the view provided by an IDS on a router would be quite different from that provided by an IDS on a host. Moreover, a single IDS may provide information in different ways to different querying IDSs because of administrative concerns. For example, an IDS may send detailed information to an administrative partner in the organization, but only inform another IDS outside the organization with some general information.

In such an environment, it is difficult to specify queries. Indeed, the same query would have to be written as many times as the number of IDSs with different system views.

In order to scale our model to a large, heterogeneous network, we propose that the queries be specified on the *expectations* of the system views (called *expected views*). Expected views are mapped to system views provided by the IDSs (called *provided views*) when queries are to be executed. Mismatch between a query that is based on an expected view and a provided view is resolved by the system automatically through the built-in expert knowledge.

System views can be predefined in terms of typical systems and typical ways that the systems provide information. For example, we may predefine a system view of the executions of shell commands which can be provided by all IDSs monitoring UNIX hosts.

Expected views can be described in terms of high-level concepts. There are several advantages of using high-level concepts. High-level concepts can hide the difference between various systems, and queries can be written on the high-level expected views once and for all. In addition, details can be hidden within high-level concepts so that the description of queries can be simpler.

A query is to get information through a system view. We say a query Q is *directly supported* by a system view if each event attribute name and dynamic predicate name used in Q appears in the view. Intuitively, if a query Q is directly supported by (R, C), then Q can be considered as defined on (R, C) even if it is originally defined on another view. Therefore, there can be multiple expected views that a query can be defined on. For example, any query defined on the expected view $(\{action, user, file\_name\}, \{same\_obj[-](x_1, x_2)\})$ can be regarded as a query on $(\{action, user, file\_name, directory\}, \{same\_obj[-](x_1, x_2)\})$ without changing any component. Among all the expected views that directly support a query, we are particularly interested in the minimal one.

DEFINITION 4.6 An expected view (R, C) is the *minimal expected view* of a query Q if Q is directly supported by (R, C), but is not directly supported by any view (R', C') where R' is a proper subset of R or C' is a proper subset of C.

The minimal expected view reflects the minimal requirement of a query. It can be formed by collecting all the event attribute names and the predicate names appearing in the conditions and the assignments.

2.2   Mismatch and Mismatch Resolution

In order to make our approach practical in a large network, we distinguish the system view on which a query is specified (i.e., the expected view) from the system view provided by the IDS (i.e., the provided view). However, this may result in situations where queries are not directly supported by the system views provided by IDSs. That is, a mismatch may occur between the minimal expected view of a query and the provided view by an IDS.

Mismatches may arise for many reasons, including misunderstandings of messages. In this work, we are interested in mismatches in the following situations, assuming that all the participating IDSs understand each other correctly (based on the work of standards like CIDF and IETF's IDEF).

- The underlying system doesn't provide the requested information through the provided view.

   There can be two reasons. First, the underlying system may not have the information. For example, a host-based IDS may not have the information about the misrouted packets. Second, the underlying system may not be willing to provide the information.

- The minimal expected view is specified in a different granularity from that of the provided view.

   Two sub-cases are of particular interest. First, the event attributes that appear in the minimal expected view and the event attributes in the provided view, though reflecting the same aspects, are in different granularities. For example, a host-based IDS may distinguish different kinds of login events, such as *telnet, rlogin, rsh, rexec,* etc.. However, a query may request information in a coarser granularity where all kinds of logins are considered the same. Second, events expected by the query and those provided by the IDS are in different levels of aggregations. For example, the three-way handshake of establishing a TCP connection may be (1) represented as three separate events (a packet with SYN flag, a packet with SYN/ACK flags, and a packet with ACK flag), (2) aggregated into one event, or (3) incorporated as a part of one TCP connection event.

The mismatch between the minimal expected view of a query and the provided view of an IDS has an impact on query evaluation. In some cases, queries can still be answered precisely, while in some other cases, approximate answers may be provided. In the worst cases, the queries may not be answered at all. In the following, we identify a number of cases for which the information expected by a query can be derived from the provided view so that mismatch can be resolved automatically. We concentrate on the cases where mismatch occurs only in event attributes, assuming the dynamic predicates required by the expected view are always in the provided view. The resolution of mismatches in dynamic predicates is interesting but will be considered in the future.

Implied View and Aggregatable View

When there exist some special connections between an expected view and a provided view, we can derive events on the expected view from those on the provided view. The expected views that can be derived from the provided view are formulated as implied views and aggregatable views.

The implied view is based on many-to-one relationships between domains of event attributes. A many-to-one relationship from domain D_1 to D_2 means that each value in D_2 is associated with zero or more values in D_1, but each value in D_1 is associated with at most one value in D_2. If a value d_1 in D_1 is associated with a value d_2 in D_2, then intuitively, d_1 implies d_2. Moreover, given two event schemas R and R', for a tuple t on R, if each attribute value of t implies a corresponding attribute value under R', then t implies a tuple t' on R', where the attribute values of t' are the implied values. Such implication between event schemas is formalized as follows.

DEFINITION 4.7 Let R and R' be two sets of event attribute names, where each attribute name is associated with a domain of values. We say that R *implies* R', denoted $R \Rightarrow R'$, if for each attribute A' in R', there exists an attribute A in R such that a many-to-one relationship is given a priori between the domains of A and A'.

When R implies R', for some tuple t in a relation of R, we can derive a tuple on R' using the many-to-one relationships between the domains of the event attributes. The following example shows such a derivation.

EXAMPLE 4.6 Suppose a network traffic monitor provides information via a provided view $(R, \emptyset)$, where $R = (app\_service, src\_ip, src\_port, dst\_ip, dst\_port)$. The domain of $app\_service$ is $\{http, ftp, telnet, tftp, DNS\}$, the domains of src_ip and dst_ip are $[1..2^{32}]$, and the domains of src_port and dst_port are $[1..2^{16}]$. Suppose a query is specified on an expected view $(R', \emptyset)$, where $R' = (transport\_service, src\_ip, dst\_ip)$ and the domain of $transport\_service$ is $\{TCP, UDP\}$. Since $http$, ftp and $telnet$ are TCP based network services, while $tftp$ and DNS are UDP based services, there exists a many-to-one relationship between the domains of $app\_service$ and $transprot\_service$. Thus, the provided view $(R, \emptyset)$ implies the expected view $(R', \emptyset)$. As shown in table 4.4, we can derive a sequence of implied events on R' from those on R.

The above definition reflects the implication between system views that is useful to derive implied events. The implication is due to the expert knowledge that can be represented as many-to-one relationships between domains of

Table 4.4. Derivation of implied events

Original events

app_service	src_ip	src_port	dst_ip	dst_port
. . .	. . .	. . .	. . .	. . .
http	129.174.142.20	4212	172.16.112.50	80
ftp	129.174.1.13	2356	129.174.142.121	21
DNS	152.169.215.104	1694	174.16.112.50	53
tftp	207.75.239.115	1234	172.16.114.50	69
. . .	. . .	. . .	. . .	. . .

Implied events

transport_service	src_ip	dst_ip
. . .	. . .	. . .
TCP	129.174.142.20	172.16.112.50
TCP	129.174.1.13	129.174.142.121
UDP	152.169.215.104	174.16.112.50
UDP	207.75.239.115	172.16.114.50
. . .	. . .	. . .

event attributes in different views. In addition to many-to-one relationship, the correspondence between simple events and compound events can also help to derive implied events.

A compound event corresponds to a set of simple events that satisfies certain conditions. For example, a TCP connection is established if the IP packets for three-way handshake are transmitted between two communication parties. In the following, we use queries to capture such correspondence.

DEFINITION 4.8 Let (R, C) and (R', C') be two system views, and $\mathcal{Q}$ be a query on (R, C). We say $\mathcal{Q}$ is a *bridging query from* (R, C) *to* (R', C') if R' is the schema of the query result and $C' \subseteq C$.

Bridging queries represent the expert knowledge that connects the system views of simple events and compound events. With a bridging query, we can derive compound events from simple events. The following example shows such a bridging query, which aggregates the IP packets for three-way hand-shake into one compound event of establishing TCP connection.

EXAMPLE 4.7 Suppose system view $(R, \emptyset)$ represents the events for IP packets carrying TCP traffic, while system view $(R', \emptyset)$ represents the TCP events in a higher-level concept. The event schema $R = \{src\_ip, src\_port, dst\_ip, dst\_port, segment\_bytes, flag\}$, and $R' = \{tcp\_event, s\_ip, s\_port, d\_ip, d\_port, bytes\}$. The domain of tcp_event is $\{establish\_conn, transmit,$

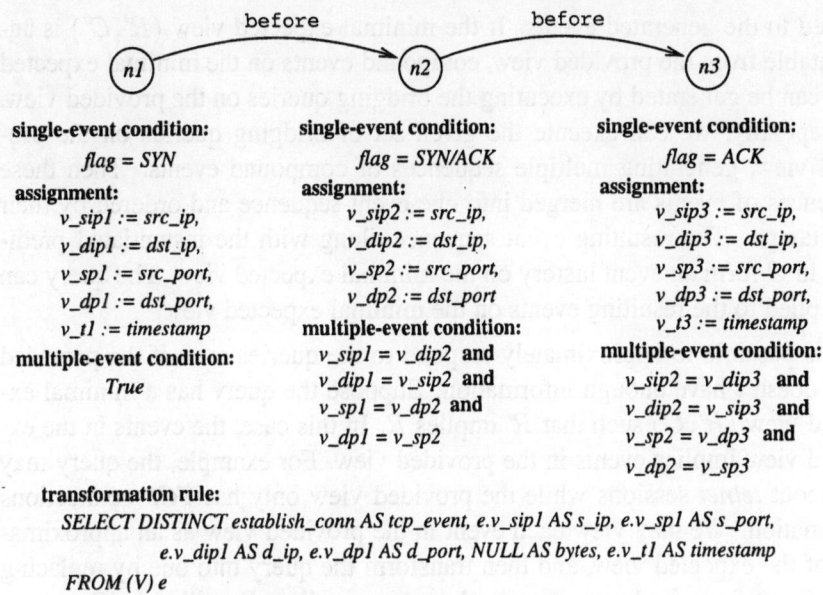

Figure 4.3. A query aggregating TCP 3-way handshake into *establish_conn* events

release_conn}, and the domains of other attributes are obvious from the attribute names. Figure 4.3 shows a bridging query from $(R, \emptyset)$ to $(R', \emptyset)$. This query aggregates each combination of three events regarding a three-way handshake into one *establish_conn* event.

We may need more than one query to aggregate simple events on one view to compound events on another. For example, there may be two additional bridging queries for the *transmit* and *release_conn* events for the two system views in example 4.7, each of which covers one kind of compound event.

DEFINITION 4.9 Let (R, C) and (R', C') be two system views. We say the system view (R', C) is *aggregatable from* (R, C) if a non-empty set of bridging queries from (R, C) to (R', C) is given a priori.

The implication and aggregation relationships between system views can be applied to resolve mismatches between the expected view of a query and the provided view by an IDS.

Let us consider a provided view (R, C) by an IDS and a query with the minimal expected view (R', C'). If the event schema R' is implied by R and the set of dynamic predicates C' is contained in C, implied events on the minimal expected view can be generated from the provided view, then the query can be applied to the generated events. If the minimal expected view (R', C') is aggregatable from the provided view, compound events on the minimal expected view can be generated by executing the bridging queries on the provided view. Conceptually, we can execute the given set of bridging queries on the provided view, generating multiple sequences of compound events. Then these sequences of events are merged into one event sequence and ordered by their timestamps. The resulting event sequence along with the instantiated predicates in C form an event history on the minimal expected view. The query can be applied to the resulting events on the minimal expected view.

It is possible to approximately respond to the queries even if the provided view doesn't have enough information. Suppose the query has a minimal expected view (R', C) such that R' implies R. In this case, the events in the expected view implies events in the provided view. For example, the query may ask about *telnet* sessions while the provided view only has *TCP* connections information. We may view each event in the provided view as an approximation of the expected view, and then transform the query into one by replacing each R' attribute in the query with the corresponding R attribute. (Constants in the query may also need to be replaced with implied values.) The transformed query is then directly supported by the provided view. Although the transformed query is just an approximation to the original one, the result of such a query may still convey some information useful to the requesting IDS.

3. Discussion

3.1 Comparison with Alternative Approaches

There are alternatives to our approach in getting specific information from other IDSs. Instead of sending structured queries, one IDS may send a piece of mobile code to the remote system. The remote IDS can then execute the mobile code, which will collect the requested information from the events exported by the remote system.

This approach is more expressive and flexible than ours. With the capability of a programming language, it can get any result that is computable from the remote event stream. However, it also has several disadvantages compared to our approach.

First, due to difficulties in program verification, it will be very difficult for the remote IDS to determine whether the mobile code performs any malicious actions. The remote IDS will have to have some strict access control mechanism to restrict the operations of the mobile code. Nevertheless, the continued discovery of security holes in Java indicates that it is difficult to ensure the executing system is safe from all threats. On the other hand, what a query requests is clear in our approach.

Second, mobile code is usually written in a programming language like Java, which is hard to manipulate and the correctness of the program is difficult to verify. On the contrary, our approach provides built-in constructs for events and has a graphical representation so that a query writer can concentrate on the semantics of the query.

A variant of this approach is to use a script language (e.g. NFR's N-code [Ranum et al., 1997]) or a database query language (e.g. SQL). This approach imposes less security risk, however, still suffers from the second disadvantage.

Another alternative is to classify the events into several classes, and the event information is sent to an IDS based on its request to the event classes (e.g., gido class in CIDF [Kahn et al., 1998a]). Since this method doesn't consider requests for structural interrelationships among events, it either requires a very complex classification (so that the structural relationships are part of the classification criteria), or unnecessary message transmission on the network cannot be avoided.

Our approach can be considered as a further step on the basis of the above classification. In addition to event classes, which can be characterized by the single-event conditions, we also consider the structural interrelationship among events (i.e., the temporal order of events and the multiple-event conditions) as well as the transformation from the original event information into the requested form.

There are also alternative formalisms to our approach. We noticed that several signature-based intrusion detection models can be modified to specify queries. Indeed, our model is modified from one of them [Lin et al., 1998]. Another interesting model is the Colored-PetriNet model [Kumar, 1995, Kumar and Spafford, 1994].

Applying the Colored PetriNet model to our problem can result in a more expressive model. Since a Colored PetriNet Automaton can model the moves of a Turing machine [Kumar, 1995], it can represent any request that is computable from the exported events. However, a Colored PetriNet Automaton is more complex and harder to manipulate. Besides, our approach can use a direct mapping to relational database queries and thus take advantage of the technical progresses in the relational database field.

3.2 Relationship with Signature-based Intrusion Detection

These exists a strong relationship between models for signature-based intrusion detection and our model. Due to this relationship, it is possible to modify the model and the software for signature-based intrusion detection for the interoperation of IDSs as we did here.

Signature-based intrusion detection (also called *misuse detection*) attempts to encode knowledge about attacks as well-defined patterns and monitors for the occurrence of these patterns [Kumar and Spafford, 1994]. The intrusion patterns are encoded as signatures, which are specifications of features, conditions, arrangements and interrelationships among events that signify intrusive activities.

Similarities exist between the signature in the context of intrusion detection, and the query in the context of interoperation of IDSs. Both of them can be considered as a set of constraints, which are tested against the event stream (e.g., the audit trail). In both cases, satisfaction of the constraints indicates the discovery of the desired information. The specifications of both consist of conditions, arrangements and structural interrelationships among events.

There are also differences between the signature-based intrusion detection and the query-based interoperation of IDSs. First, for the purpose of intrusion detection, the main concern is whether the intrusive activity occurs or not, while for the interoperation of IDSs, we care more about the flexible manipulation of the information associated with events. Second, the *existence* of certain events may be enough for the purpose of intrusion detection, while it is important for a query to get the *complete* information. For example, if one IDS requests the number of failed login attempts at a remote system, it should have the result about all the failed login events.

Because of the similarity between the signature and the query, we may generate query results by modifying the software for signature-based intrusion detection. Since many IDSs currently support signature-based approach, this method can save much effort thanks to the potential reuse of the existing software modules.

3.3 Implementation Issues

Our model is built on the implicit assumption that all the IDSs have common agreement about both the syntax and the semantics of the interchanged messages. This assumption may not be satisfied if the interoperation is between heterogeneous IDSs. Nevertheless, this assumption is always a premise if we would like different IDSs to share information. We believe that the communication between heterogeneous IDSs will not be an obstacle if some common format is adopted.

Since different IDSs may provide different system views, and queries are specified on the basis of the expectation of the system views, it would be necessary to predefine typical system views for typical systems. In addition, relationships between system views should be provided to reduce the amount of work involved in mismatch resolution. Implications of event attributes can be provided, and implications of event schemas can be derived from the combination of event attributes in the schema. Bridging queries should be provided to link system views at different aggregation levels.

Queries can be predefined or specified by the administrator on some occasions. To specify a query, the query writer should have two kinds of information: (1) what I need from the remote IDS, that is, the expected view of the remote IDS; and (2) what is to be requested from the remote IDS, that is, the set of constraints and the transformation rule for the query. The former information will be ready for the query writer if the system views are predefined and classified, while the latter is up to the writer's understanding about his (her) goal.

Query templates can be used to further reduce the work involved in the specification of queries. A query template specifies a request for information on the basis of some parameters. When interoperate with other IDSs, we replace the parameters with constants and send out the instantiated query. Libraries of query templates may be published and shared among many systems.

One way to take advantage of query templates (and the query facility) is to use them along with some triggering mechanism such as rule-base expert system. For example, we may associate appropriate query templates with the rules in a rule-based expert system. When these rules are fired due to certain events, the associated templates can be instantiated using the event attributes and sent to other IDR components. The automatic generation and processing of IDR queries is an interesting topic; however, we do not cover it in this dissertation but consider it as future work.

In order to prevent attackers from misusing the query facility (e.g., stealing secret information by posing a query, or tricking an IDS to perform meaningless operations), the cooperating IDSs should use strong cryptographic techniques to authenticate each other and ensure the integrity and the confidentiality of the messages transmitted between them. However, this problem is out of the scope of this dissertation.

Chapter 5

EXTENDING COMMON INTRUSION DETECTION FRAMEWORK (CIDF) TO SUPPORT QUERIES

In this chapter, we apply the formal model that we developed in Chapter 4 to provide a query facility for Common Intrusion Detection Framework (CIDF).

CIDF is the result of an on-going work that aims at enabling different intrusion detection and response (IDR) components to interoperate and share information [Feiertag et al., 2000a, Kahn et al., 1998a, Kahn et al., 1998b, Porras et al., 1998, Tung, 1998]. The CIDF working group was formed as a collaboration among DARPA funded IDR projects. Although CIDF provides an infrastructure and language support that allows an IDR component to understand the information that is sent by a remote IDR component, it does not contain a facility for an IDR component to request specific information from another component. As we discussed earlier, the lack of such a facility may result in inefficient communication between IDR components. In this chapter, we propose an extension to the common intrusion specification language (CISL), the language adopted by CIDF, on the basis of the formal framework that we proposed in Chapter ch:query. The extension allows IDR components to specify requests for particular information from other IDR components.

As an application of the formal model developed in Chapter 4, the extension describes requests for particular information in terms of patterns. A pattern specifies the characteristics of the information in which the requesting IDR component is interested. Based on S-expressions (which is the language construct adopted by CISL), patterns are described using "wild-card terms" that stand for SIDs (semantic identifiers) or data values, and conditions that these wild-card terms must satisfy. Basically, each pattern gives a set of S-expressions that match the pattern. Together with the semantics assigned by CIDF to the "words" in CISL, patterns allow CIDF components to precisely express requests.

A component that receives a request is expected to find the information that matches the pattern, instantiate the wild-cards in the pattern according to the information, and return the resulting message composed from the instantiation. Optionally, the requesting component may specify the format for the responding message.

Note that the extension proposed in this chapter is independent of the message transmission model, which can be either a push or a pull model. Indeed, the extended CISL not only enables an IDR component to send queries to other components, but also allows it to set up traps at remote systems.

The rest of the chapter is organized as follows. Section 5.1 briefly describes the background of CIDF and CISL. Section 5.2 discusses our extension for specifying requests using S-patterns. Section 5.3 discusses some implementation issues involved in the deployment of the request facility.

1. Background

CIDF is a framework that aims at interoperation and software reuse among IDR systems [Feiertag et al., 2000a, Kahn et al., 1998a, Kahn et al., 1998b, Porras et al., 1998, Tung, 1998]. CIDF views IDR systems as consisting of discrete components that communicate via message passing. Four kinds of IDR components are envisaged: Event Generators (E-boxes), Event Analyzers (A-boxes), Event Databases (D-boxes) and Response Units (R-boxes). An event generator obtains events from the larger computational environment outside the IDR system; an event analyzer receives information from other components, analyzes them, and returns the analysis result; an event database stores information; and a response unit takes actions (e.g., killing a process) on behalf of other components.

Data exchanged among CIDF components is specified in the form of *generalized intrusion detection objects (gidos)* which are described in the Common Intrusion Specification Language (CISL). A gido encodes an occurrence of a particular event that happened at a particular time, a conclusion about a set of events, or an instruction to carry out an action.

CIDF components communicate over a three-layered architecture, which consists of the gido layer, the message layer and the negotiated transport layer. Data to be exchanged is first encoded in gidos. Then gidos are encapsulated in messages. Finally, messages are sent over a transport mechanism negotiated between the communicating components.

The purpose of the gido layer is to allow components to have a common understanding of the semantics of the data they send to each other. As the language to specify gidos, CISL provides a rich, extensible format with defined semantics so that the information being exchanged can be described. We will describe CISL in further detail in section 5.1.1.

The message layer is concerned with security, efficiency and reliability of the communication. Message format and message processing procedures are defined to ensure secure, reliable and efficient communication among CIDF components.

The transport mechanism is not part of the CIDF specification. However, a protocol based on the reliable UDP is selected as the default transport protocol. Other transport layer protocols may be used after a negotiation procedure.

CIDF also specifies how IDR components communicate with each other. A directory service based on the lightweight directory access protocol, called *matchmaking service* or *matchmaker*, provides a mechanism for CIDF components to advertise themselves and to locate communication partners with which they can share information.

1.1   Common Intrusion Specification Language

CISL is proposed to specify events, analysis results and responses among CIDF components [Feiertag et al., 2000a, Kahn et al., 1998b]. CISL is based on a Lisp-like general language construct, called S-expressions. S-expressions are syntactic constructs for nested groupings of tags and data, where the grouping is done with parentheses. For example,

```
(HostName 'ten.ada.net')
```

is an S-expression that groups two terms, HostName and 'ten.ada.net'. The term immediately after the first left parenthesis of an S-expression (e.g., HostName in the example) is the *tag* of the S-expression, and the terms after the tag and before the matching right parenthesis (e.g., 'ten.ada.net') are the data values grouped with the tag. The data values grouped with a tag are called the argument of the tag. We also say an S-expression is headed by *x* if *x* is the tag of the S-expression. The argument grouped with a tag can be not only simple constants, but also S-expressions (i.e., nested S-expressions).

Tags are assigned with well-defined semantics in CIDF to help the interpretation of the data grouped with them. These tags are called Semantic IDentifiers, or SIDs. In the example above, HostName is an SID with the assigned semantics that the string 'ten.ada.net' should be interpreted as a hostname.

SIDs are divided into several groups. The SIDs that denote actions, recommendations or state descriptions are called *verb SIDs*. An S-expression that has at least one verb SID appearing in it is called a *sentence*. A verb SID takes as its argument a sequence of S-expressions that tells the various aspects about the sentence. For example, in the following S-expression, Delete is a verb SID that denotes the action of *deletion*.

```
(Delete
     (Location
          (Time '15:30:34 10 June 1999')
```

```
        )
        (Initiator
            (UserName 'Joe')
        )
        (Source
            (Filename '/etc/passwd')
            (Owner
                (UserName 'root')
            )
        )
    )
```

The SIDs that govern the information about the "players" associated with a verb are called *role SIDs*. A role SID takes as argument a sequence of S-expressions that identify or describe the entity playing the indicated role. An S-expression headed by a role SID is called a *role clause*. In the S-expression above, Location, Initiator, Source and Owner are all role SIDs.

There are two special kinds of role SIDs. A role SID that does not describe an object, but locates a verb SID or modifies its meaning is called an *adverb SID*. For example, in the S-expression above, Location is an adverb SID that governs the information about the the context of the deletion event. A role SID that can only occur directly under another role SID (i.e., the S-expression headed by the former role SID is an argument of the latter role SID) is called an *attribute SIDs*. For example, in the S-expression shown above, Owner is an attribute SID that governs the information about the owner of the deleted file. Attribute SIDs describe an entity that has a relation to another entity rather than to the whole sentence.

An SID that can only take a constant as its argument is called an *atom SIDs*. For example, in the S-expression shown above, Time, UserName and Filename are all atom SIDs. Atom SIDs can only appear inside role clauses. Atom SIDs give property values while verb and role SIDs organize the structure of the values. An S-expression headed by an atom SID is called an *atom clause*, or sometimes an *SID-data pair*.

There are two special atom SIDs, *ReferAs* and *ReferTo*. They are collectively called *referent SIDs*. Referent SIDs allow one to link two or more sentences together (or two or more parts of the same sentence). The SID ReferAs labels a role clause or a sentence, and the SID ReferTo refers to the role clause or the sentence using the label.

The SIDs that can join sentences together are called *conjunction SIDs* (i.e., each S-expression in the argument of a conjunction SID must contain at least one verb SID). Conjunction SIDs state the relationship among sentences.

For detailed definition of SIDs, please refer to the CISL document [Feiertag et al., 2000a].

2.   A Query Facility for CIDF

For the purpose of efficiency, an IDR component needs to describe specifically what they would like to request from other components. In this section, we will model such requests by providing a query facility for CIDF.

Our extension is to add new SIDs and language constructs so that a CIDF component may specify requests using the extended language. The specification of a query is separated into two parts: a condition that the information of interest must satisfy and an optional specification of the particular information that must be returned to the requesting component. We first use special S-expressions called *S-patterns* to capture the former part, then describe the latter part either implicitly with the patterns or explicitly with specifications.

2.1   S-Patterns

An S-pattern is an S-expression with "wild-card terms" that stand for certain kinds of SIDs or data values, and conditions that these wild-card terms must satisfy. Similar to other pattern representations (e.g., regular expressions), an S-pattern is a syntactic notation for describing a set of S-expressions. For example, the following S-expression is an S-pattern, in which the SID AVerb is a wild-card SID that stands for all verb SIDs.

```
(AVerb
    (Initiator
        (UserName 'Joe')
    )
)
```

The two SIDs, Initiator and UserName, are as defined in the CISL specification, and 'Joe' is the data value grouped with UserName. This pattern represents the set of all S-expressions that have the above form but with AVerb replaced with a particular verb SID, e.g., the S-expression derived from above by replacing AVerb with Delete.

Given the semantics assigned to the SIDs, an S-pattern expresses the information that an IDR component may be interested in. For example, the aforementioned S-expression represents all the actions or responses that are initiated by the user whose user name is Joe.

There are two kinds of wild-card terms, wild-card SIDs and wild-card data values. We introduce several wild-card SIDs, each of which represents a class of SIDs (e.g., AVerb is a wild-card SID representing verb SIDs). To allow conditions refer to the SID that takes the place of a wild-card SID, we also introduce naming SIDs for wild-card SIDs so that we can give a wild-card SID a name and later use the name to specify the conditions.

A different approach is used to represent wild-card data values due to the restriction imposed by the CISL (which will be discussed later). We introduce a couple of *escape SIDs* such that when they take atom clauses as arguments (recall that data values only appear in atom clauses), the data values will be reinterpreted as wild-card data values. To facilitate the use of wild-card data values in conditions, the escape SIDs also assign names to the wild-card data values.

We describe conditions with predicates and logical combinations of predicates. Accordingly, we introduce SIDs that stand for predicates and logical operations to specify the conditions. Predicates determine the relationship among their arguments, and logical operations allow representation of complex relationships by combinations of predicates.

In summary, we add the following kinds of SIDs to support the specification of patterns.

- wild-card SIDs: `AVerb`, `ARole`, etc.

- naming SIDs for wild-card SIDs: `SIDReferAs` and `SIDReferTo`

- escape SIDs: `ValueReferAs` and `ValueReferTo`

- predicate SIDs: `EqualTo`, `LessThan`, etc.

- logical operation SIDs: `LogicalAnd`, `LogicalOr` and `LogicalNot`

- other SIDs: `Condition`, `Query` and `SIDValue`

In the following, we explain these SIDs in further detail.

Wild-card SIDs

A wild-card SID is essentially a variable which stands for any SID that can be placed at that position. We have seen an example using the wild-card SID `AVerb` at the beginning of section 5.2.1.

The following wild-card SIDs are added to the CISL to support S-patterns: `AVerb`, `ARole`, `AnAdverb`, `AnAttribute`, `AConjunction`, and `AnAtom`. They are wild-cards for the corresponding kinds of SIDs. `AVerb` is a verb SID that stands for any verb SID other than `AVerb`. It can be placed in an S-expression as a normal verb SID and represents any verb SID other than `AVerb`. `ARole` is a role SID that stands for any role SID other than `ARole`. It can be placed in an S-expression as a normal role SID and represents any role SID other than `ARole`. The wild-card SIDs `AnAdverb`, `AnAttribute`, `AConjunction` and `AnAtom` are similarly defined.

Naming SIDs and `SIDValue`

Two naming SIDs, `SIDReferAs` and `SIDReferTo`, are introduced to facilitate the use of wild-card SIDs in conditions. Following the convention of CISL, they are atom SIDs that take unsigned long integers as arguments. `SIDReferAs` is usually placed under a wild-card SID such that the S-expression headed by the `SIDReferAs` is in the argument of the wild-card SID. We use `SIDReferAs` to give names to wild-card SIDs, and use `SIDReferTo` to make reference to names.

For convenience of presentation, however, we will use "symbolic names" for the data values grouped with the naming SIDs hereafter. They can be easily transformed to unsigned integers.

Another SID, `SIDValue`, is introduced to facilitate the comparisons involving wild-card SIDs and "constant" SIDs. `SIDValue` is an atom SID that takes a valid SID as its argument. It instructs that its argument be interpreted as an SID. For example, the S-expression (`SIDValue Delete`) means that `Delete` is an SID.

The following S-expression shows an example of the naming SIDs for wild-card SIDs.

```
(AVerb
    (Initiator
        (UserName 'Joe')
    )
    (SIDReferAs var_verb)
    (Condition
        (NotEqual
            (SIDReferTo var_verb)
            (SIDValue Delete)
        )
    )
)
```

The clause (`SIDReferAs var_verb`) gives the name `var_verb` to the wild-card SID AVerb, and (`SIDReferTo var_verb`) later uses the wild-card SID by making reference to `var_verb`. Here `NotEqual` is a predicate SID which determines whether the verb SID represented by `var_verb` is SID `Delete` or not, and `Condition` is the SID that governs the conditions for the pattern. Thus, together with the semantics assigned to the SIDs, this S-expression represents the S-pattern for all the actions or responses initiated by user `'Joe'` except for deletion. We will explain predicate SIDs and the SID `Condition` in more detail later.

`SIDReferAs`/`SIDReferTo` SIDs are different from `ReferAs`/`ReferTo`. The SIDs `ReferAs`/`ReferTo` link roles or sentences represented by the corresponding S-expressions, while `SIDReferAs`/`SIDReferTo` refer to wild-card SIDs.

Escape SIDs

Because of the restriction imposed by the CISL, we cannot use the same naming mechanism as we used for wild-card SIDs. Since sentences specified in CISL are intended to be encoded in binary forms and some types of data values are assigned a fixed-length field (e.g., `IPV4Checksum` is a 16-bit integer), we cannot use a special data value as a wild-card term (otherwise, we won't be able to represent some data value, for example, a checksum of an IP packet). Thus, we introduce a couple of escape SIDs such that when they take atom clauses as their arguments, the data values will be reinterpreted as wild-card data values.

Two escape SIDs, `ValueReferAs` and `ValueReferTo`, are introduced to represent wild-card data values and assign names to the data values.

An escape SID takes atom clauses as its argument, and causes the data values grouped with the atom SID to be interpreted as "names" for wild-card data values. Also, within an S-expression headed by an escape SID, an atom SID takes an unsigned long integer as argument (for convenience of presentation again, we shall use symbolic names instead of integers). For example, the S-expression

```
(ValueReferAs
    (UserName var_uname)
)
```

makes var_uname being interpreted as a reference to a possible user name. An S-expression headed by an escape SID is called an *escape clause*, and can be used as an atom clause.

As `SIDReferAs` and `SIDReferTo`, `ValueReferAs` gives a name to a data value that is grouped with an atom SID, and `ValueReferTo` catches this value by making a reference to the name. For example, in the following S-expression that represents an S-pattern of all the delete actions initiated by users other than Joe, the possible value of `UserName` under the `Initiator` role clause is given a name var_uname, and later `ValueReferTo` makes a reference to this value under the `NotEqual` SID.

```
(Delete
    (Initiator
        (ValueReferAs
            (UserName var_uname)
        )
    )
```

```
· (Condition
     (NotEqual
          (ValueReferTo
               (UserName var_uname)
          )
          (UserName 'Joe')
     )
  )
)
```

Predicate SIDs

Predicate SIDs are introduced to help state conditions for patterns in S-expressions. Predicate SIDs are role SIDs. A predicate SID takes as its argument role clauses, atom clauses and (or) escape clauses, representing the relationship among them.

An S-expression headed by a predicate SID is called a *predicate clause*, or more specifically a *simple predicate clause*. A predicate clause is expected to return True or False according to whether the relationship holds or not.

The following S-expression shows an example of predicate clause that represents whether the host denoted by var_host is in the domain 'ada.net'. Here we assume that var_host is defined by ValueReferAs somewhere else.

```
(HostInDomain
     (ValueReferTo
          (FQHostName var_host)
     )
     (DomainName 'ada.net')
)
```

Predicate SIDs are important for the expressiveness of the extended language. Since the original language was not developed for specifying requests, no SIDs pertaining to request are included in the language specification. To fully support CIDF components to ask queries, extensive work is needed to determine what predicate SIDs should be provided. We will not give a complete list for predicate SIDs in this dissertation, but consider it as future work. The predicate SIDs used in the examples of this dissertation are HostInDomain, NotEqual and LessThan, whose semantics are explained along with the examples.

Logical Operation SIDs

Logical operation SIDs are used to represent complex conditions by logically combining simple predicate clauses. Logical operation SIDs are role SIDs that represent logical operations. Corresponding to the three logical operations AND, OR and NOT, three logical operation SIDs, `LogicalAnd`, `LogicalOr` and `LogicalNot`, are used.

A logical operation SID takes as its argument a sequence of predicate clauses (in the case of `LogicalNot`, only one S-expression is allowed as its argument), representing the result of applying the corresponding logical operation to the argument. An S-expression headed by a logical operation SID is also called a predicate clause, or more specifically a *complex predicate clause*. Therefore, logical operation SIDs along with predicate SIDs can recursively express complex conditions. For example, the following S-expression shows a condition that `var_verb` is not `Delete` and `var_host` is within the `'ada.net'` domain. Here we assume that `var_verb` and `var_host` have been defined.

```
(LogicalAnd
    (NotEqual
        (SIDReferTo var_verb)
        (SIDValue Delete)
    )
    (HostInDomain
        (ValueReferTo
            (FQHostName var_host)
        )
        (DomainName 'ada.net')
    )
)
```

SIDs `Condition` and `Query`

The SIDs `Condition` and `Query` are used to organize S-expressions for conditions and patterns, respectively. The SID `Condition` is introduced to govern the S-expressions that describe the conditions that must be satisfied by the wild-card terms. The `Condition` SID takes as argument an S-expressions headed by predicate SIDs or logical operation SIDs (i.e., a predicate clause). An S-expression headed by the `Condition` SID is called a *condition clause*. To make conditions specific, we require that each condition clause be placed directly under a verb or `AVerb` SID, meaning that the condition must be satisfied when the action, description of analysis result or response corresponding to the verb SID occurs.

The SID `Query` is introduced to govern the S-expressions that describe a pattern. `Query` SID is a conjunction SID that takes as its argument a sequence of sentences. An S-expression headed by `Query` SID is called a *query sentence*.

With the SIDs introduced earlier, CIDF components are provided with support for specification of S-patterns. The following example shows a complete S-pattern.

EXAMPLE 5.1 Suppose a component wants to know from what IP address and port a user with user name 'Joe' telnets to the host having IP address '10.0.0.3'. The component can specify this request using the following pattern.

```
(Query
   (Login
      (Initiator
         (UserName 'Joe')
      )
      (Session
         (ValueReferAs
            (SourceIPV4Address s_IP)
            (TCPSourcePort s_port)
         )
         (DestinationIPV4Address '10.0.0.3')
         (TCPDestinationPort 23)
      )
      (Condition
         (NotEqual
            (ValueReferTo
               (SourceIPV4Address s_IP)
            )
            (DestinationIPV4Address '10.0.0.3')
         )
      )
   )
)
```

2.2   Format of Returning Message

With the extension introduced above, a CIDF component is able to describe its interest as S-patterns. However, S-patterns are not specific enough to express the exact request of a component. In other words, it is not clear what should be included in the reply to a query and how the information should be arranged. As a result, it is still possible that a requesting component gets unnecessary messages or misses important information. Thus, additional mechanism is needed in order to provide a sufficient solution.

There are alternative ways to solve this problem. The content and the arrangement of the reply (i.e., the format of the returning message) can be specified either implicitly or explicitly in the request. In the following, we will discuss them respectively.

Implicit Request for Returning Message

The information that must be returned can be specified implicitly. When a component finds the information that matches a request, it is required to instantiate all the wild-card terms in the request using the information and return the resulting S-expression. This approach basically assigns a "returning all" semantic to a query sentence.

In order to have the requested information, a component has to list the particular aspects of information as wild-card SIDs or wild-card data values.

For example, with the assigned "returning all" semantic, the query sentence shown in example 1 specifies a request for all the session information about user Joe's telnet sessions. The requesting component can directly send the query sentence to the event analyzer that monitors the host. Suppose the event analyzer that receives the query does find a telnet session to '10.0.0.3' initiated by user 'Joe' and the source IP address and the source port number are '129.174.40.15' and 6543, respectively. It will instantiate the wild-card data values s_IP and s_port in the above query and return the following S-expression.

```
(Login
    (Initiator
        (UserName 'Joe')
    )
    (Session
        (SourceIPV4Address '129.174.40.15')
        (TCPSourcePort 6543)
        (DestinationIPV4Address '10.0.0.3')
        (TCPDestinationPort 23)
    )
    (Condition
        (NotEqual
            (SourceIPV4Address '129.174.40.15')
            (DestinationIPV4Address '10.0.0.3')
        )
    )
)
```

The advantage of this approach is its simplicity. By assigning the "returning all" semantic to a query sentence, it doesn't need any additional mechanisms. In addition, the relationships represented by the conditions in queries are also kept in the returning message. Thus, the returning messages are complete in the sense that all the related constraints are contained in the message.

However, some information may be redundant in the returning message. Some part of the query may be presented to specify the conditions that the requested information should satisfy, and may not be of interest to the requesting component. If we use this approach, these parts will have to be returned by the requested component.

Explicit Request for Returning Message

Alternatively, we can specify explicitly what should be returned and how the information is arranged. We introduce an additional component into a query, which arranges the format of returning messages.

A new SID, Format, is introduced to govern S-expressions that specify the format. Format is a conjunction SID that takes sentences as argument. It is always placed directly under the SID Query, representing the request by the query for particular messages. S-expressions under the SID Format are described using constants as well as references to wild-cards and data values that appear in the pattern of the same query. An S-expression headed by the SID Format is called a *format sentence*.

A format sentence describes the requested aspect of the information. When there is information that matches the S-pattern, related aspects are extracted and described in S-expression according to the format sentence.

For example, with the explicit approach, the query about the telnet session shown in example 1 can be specified as follows.

```
(Query
   (Login
      (Initiator
         (UserName 'Joe')
      )
      (Session
         (ValueReferAs
            (SourceIPV4Address s_IP)
            (TCPSourcePort s_port)
         )
         (DestinationIPV4Address '10.0.0.3')
         (TCPDestinationPort 23)
      )
      (Condition
         (NotEqual
            (ValueReferTo
               (SourceIPV4Address s_IP)
            )
            (DestinationIPV4Address '10.0.0.3')
         )
      )
```

```
      )
      (Format
         (Login
            (Session
               (ValueReferAs
                  (SourceIPV4Address s_IP)
                  (TCPSourcePort s_port)
               )
            )
         )
      )
   )
```

When the event analyzer finds the corresponding telnet session information, it will arrange the session information according to the S-expression under the SID Format and return the following responding message.

```
(Login
   (Session
      (SourceIPV4Address '129.174.40.15')
      (TCPSourcePort 6543)
   )
)
```

Using the explicit approach, the responding message can be shorter than when the implicit approach is used, since at least those parts that specify conditions in the pattern can be omitted from the responding message. This will save network bandwidth and processing time for the reply.

However, the requesting messages usually become larger because of the explicit specification of the general form of responding messages. In addition, the requesting components should be able to link responding messages to requesting ones. In other words, the requesting components must know which responding message replies to which requesting message. Here we assume that there exist other mechanisms that link the corresponding requesting and responding messages together. A simple solution could be embedding in the reply the identifier of the requesting message.

2.3   An Example – Tracing Suspicious Users

We conclude this section with an example of tracing suspicious users. Tracing techniques have been studied by various research groups and some solutions specialized for this problem have been proposed (e.g., thumbprinting [Staniford-Chen and Heberlein, 1995]). Here we show how we can achieve the same purpose through the cooperation of CIDF components that communicate using the extended CISL. The language extension is certainly not limited to this problem.

Suppose the Event Analyzer monitoring host *A* detects a suspicious user who remotely logged in from host *B* and wants to trace the origin of this user. The Event Analyzer discovers that the user was connected from host *B* to host *A* through a telnet session beginning at 14:45:36 on May 17 1999, and the telnet session is carried over a TCP connection from IP address '10.0.0.2' port 4321 to IP address '10.0.0.1' port 23 ('10.0.0.1' and '10.0.0.2' are IP addresses of host *A* and *B*, respectively). Then the Event Analyzer for host *A* can start tracing by posing the following query to the Event Analyzer for host *B* instead of getting all login-related events from the corresponding Event Generator.

```
(Query
  (Login
    (Location
      (ValueReferAs
        (Time login_time)
      )
    )
    (Initiator
      (ValueReferAs
        (HostName src_host)
      )
    )
    (Session
      (ValueReferAs
        (SourceIPV4Address s_IP)
        (TCPSourcePort s_Port)
        (DestinationIPV4Address d_IP)
        (TCPDestinationPort d_Port)
      )
      (ReferAs first_session)
    )
    (Account
      (HostName B)
    )
    (Condition
      (NotEqual
        (ValueReferTo
          (HostName src_host)
        )
        (HostName B)
      )
```

```
            )
        (ReferAs first_login)
    )
    (Login
        (Location
            (Time '14:45:36 17 May 1999')
        )
        (Session
            (SourceIPV4Address '10.0.0.2')
            (TCPSourcePort 4321)
            (DesinationIPV4Address '10.0.0.1')
            (TCPDestinationPort 23)
            (Ancestor
                (ReferTo first_session)
            )
        )
        (Condition
            (LessThan
                (ValueReferTo
                    (Time login_time)
                )
                (Time '14:45:36 17 May 1999')
            )
        )
    )
    (Format
        (ReferTo first_login)
    )
)
```

Informally, this query asks: From where and when did the suspicious user log into host B, given the clue that he (or she) telneted to host A through a TCP connection from IP address '10.0.0.2' port 4321 to IP '10.0.0.1' port 23 at time '14:45:36 on May 17 1999?

In the query sentence, the Query SID takes as argument three sentences. The first sentence is headed by a Login SID, representing the login event that the suspicious user logged into host B remotely. The references to login time and the parameters for the TCP session expresses the interest of the requesting component, and the condition explains that the initiating host should be one different from host B. The second sentence is also headed by a Login SID, representing the login event that the suspicious user remotely logged into host A from host B. The Location clause and the Session clause specify the login time and TCP connection that carried the login event, respectively. The attribute clause headed by `Ancestor`, which is under the `Session` SID, also requires that this session must be started within the session of the first login event (i.e., the session referred by `first_session` is an ancestor session of the second session). The condition clause of the second sentence explains that the first login event should be before the second one. The third sentence states that the returning message should be in the same form as the first login sentence, which is denoted by the reference `first_login`.

Suppose the Event Analyzer for host *B* discovers that the suspicious user logged into *B* from host `'another.hop.com'` at time `'14:40:04'` on May 17 1999, and the TCP connection that carried this remote login was from `'129.174.142.177'` port 1234 to `'10.0.0.2'` port 23 (i.e., a telnet session). Then the Event Analyzer will return a responding message as follows (according to the format sentence in the requesting message).

```
(Login
    (Location
        (Time '14:40:04 17 May 1999')
    )
    (Initiator
        (HostName 'another.hop.com')
    )
    (Session
        (SourceIPV4Address '129.174.40.15')
        (TCPSourcePort 1234)
        (DestinationIPV4Address '10.0.0.2')
        (TCPDestinationPort 23)
    )
    (Account
        (HostName B)
    )
    (Condition
        (NotEqual
            (HostName 'another.hop.com')
            (HostName B)
        )
    )
)
```

After receiving the responding message, the Event Analyzer for host *A* may send the Event Analyzer for host `'another.hop.com'` a similar query sentence with the new information to determine the origin of the user. This process may continue until the origin of the user is found.

3. Impact on CIDF

By extending CISL, we add a new facility into CIDF, namely specification of request for particular information. CIDF components are given a mechanism to specify requests for selected information so that message processing effort, storage capacity and network bandwidth can be saved. However, it also imposes new requirements on CIDF components.

In order to take advantage of the new functionality, a CIDF component has to decide what to request according to its needs, and describes them in correct forms. This requires that the component not only understand the language used to describe requests (i.e., CISL), but also send right requesting messages to the right partners when necessary. This seems to be a strong requirement. However, this requirement can be satisfied by classifying typical situations and arranging possible requesting messages ahead of time. Rule-based expert systems may help to generate requests automatically. Of course, requests may also be improvised by system administrators or site security officers to handle exceptional situations.

When cooperating with components from which requesting messages have been received, a CIDF component should understand the requesting messages correctly, find the necessary information, and send back the replying messages in the CISL. This requires that the component have some mechanisms to find the requested information. This requirement is outside the scope of the original CIDF. One possible way to generate reply for a query is to take advantage of the signature-based intrusion detection techniques, which are well studied and widely adopted [Ilgun et al., 1995, Kumar, 1995, Kumar and Spafford, 1994, Lin et al., 1998]. Since both queries in our language extension and the signature-based intrusion detection techniques are based on patterns, it is possible to translate a query in the extended CISL into a description in a certain signature-based intrusion detection model, find the answer using existing intrusion detection software modules (which is possibly modified), and translate the result back to description in the CISL.

More SIDs than those described in this dissertation may be needed for CIDF components to specify requests. Indeed, the SIDs introduced in the previous section are the minimum set of SIDs that provide the language support for specifying requests. Since the original language specification is developed for CIDF components to make statements about events, analysis results and responses, the SIDs may not be enough for making queries. For example, there is no SIDs that direct a CIDF component to collect statistics for certain events.

Determining additional SIDs that are needed for queries will involve extensive exploration of CIDF components' requirements. We don't discuss this issue in this dissertation but consider it as future work.

In this chapter, we present a model to represent distributed attacks based
on the concept of system view presented in Chapter 3. However, instead of
developing a completely new model, we extend a model named ARMD [Lin
et al., 1998, Lin, 1998], which was developed for host-based intrusion detection. There are several other models that could be used instead of ARMD, including rule based languages (e.g., P-BEST [Lindqvist and Porras, 1999] and
RUSSEL [Mounji et al., 1995]), the State Transition Analysis Tool (STAT) [Il-
gun et al., 1995, Vigna and Kermmerer, 1998, Vigna and Kemmerer, 1999],
and the Colored Petri Automata (CPA) [Kumar, 1995, Kumar and Spafford,
1994].

The main reason that we build our model on the basis of ARMD is due to its
simplicity. ARMD is expressive enough to represent event patterns with partial order among them. Since we use an abstraction-based approach, in which
detailed information is usually hidden by system views, it's unlikely that we
have attack patterns that cannot be expressed as partial order event patterns.
Moreover, our goal is distributed intrusion detection; event patterns that are
more complex than partial order event patterns will introduce substantial computation, communication and storage overhead, and thus will not be practical
in reality.

In our model, distributed attacks (or other events to be monitored) are represented as distributed event patterns called *signatures* on the basis of system
views. With system views hiding the heterogeneity of the distributed systems,
the signatures can represent the attacks in a generic way so that the signatures
apply to different types of systems in spite of their differences. For example,
with a system view hiding the differences between failed logins on different
types of systems (e.g., Windows, UNIX, or mainframe), the signatures based
on this system view can apply to all these systems. Moreover, to make this

representation suitable for large distributed systems, we further allow system views to be derived from signatures, and thus allows hierarchical specification of signatures for distributed attacks.

1. Misuse Signature

In this section, we present an extension to the abstraction-based misuse detection model proposed in ARMD [Lin, 1998, Lin et al., 1998]. ARMD is a host-based misuse detection system that provides a high-level, abstraction-based language for describing portable misuse signatures. (For brevity, we refer to both the system and the abstraction-based language used by the system as ARMD when it is clear from the context.)

In order to extend to distributed systems, the following issues need to be addressed. First, there are usually more than one system in a distributed system. ARMD's single-system viewpoint is not adequate to describe attacks occurring in such an environment. Second, ARMD assumes that events are atomic and do not overlap in time. This is reasonable for host audit trail; however, this assumption is usually not true in a distributed environment, where there could be concurrent events that overlap in time. Third, in a distributed environment, it is usually necessary to coordinate different IDSs in order to detect distributed attacks effectively and efficiently. However, ARMD and almost all the existing signature-based models do not provide such support.

Misuse signatures are event patterns that represent intrusive activities across multiple systems. On the basis of the system views, which are abstract representations of the underlying systems, a misuse signature is defined as a pattern of events on these system views. Specifically, a signature is a labeled directed graph. Each node in the graph corresponds to an abstract event on a particular system view, and each labeled arc to a qualitative temporal relationship between the two nodes (abstract events) involved in the arc. Events matched to the nodes must satisfy certain conditions, which are built into the model by associating a *timed condition* with each node.

There are two kinds of abstract events, *positive events* and *negative events*, due to their different "roles" in attacks. Positive events are the events that are necessary and critical for an attack. In other words, positive events are those necessary steps that lead to the compromise of a system. Let us look at the Mitnick attack described in [Northcutt, 1999]. In order to attack host B, the attacker first initiates a SYN flooding attack to prevent a TCP port of host A, which is trusted by B, from accepting any connection requests. (See [Schuba et al., 1997] for detailed information about SYN flooding attack.) During the SYN flooding attack, the attacker tries to establish a TCP connection to B pretending (by IP spoofing) to be from the port being flooded. If the attacker succeeds, he can do whatever host B allows host A to do since the attacking computer is mistaken for A. In this attack, the SYN flooding attack against host

A and the TCP connection to host *B* from the attacking computer are positive events, because the attack will not succeed without these two events.

However, the existence of positive events does not always imply an attack. For example, even if we observe two positive events, a SYN flooding attack against host *A* in the network traffic and a TCP connection from host *A* to host *B* on host *B* during the SYN flooding attack, they do not constitute a Mitnick attack if the TCP connection is indeed initiated from host *A* (rather than from the attacking computer). In other words, if we also observe the same TCP connection on host *A*, then the TCP connection is just a normal connection during the SYN flooding attack rather than a part of the Mitnick attack. We call the TCP connection observed on host *A* a negative event, which serves as counter evidence of attacks. Thus, negative events are such events that if they coexist with the positive events, the positive events do not constitute an attack.

Negative events have appeared in different forms in other models. For example, CPA uses (negative) invariant to specify what *must not* happen during an attack, that is, the specified attack does not occur if the associated invariant is violated (matched) [Kumar, 1995, Kumar and Spafford, 1994]. Negative events are important to reduce false alarms; however, they should be used with cautions. The signature writer should be certain that the existence of negative events indeed indicates the non-existence of attacks. Otherwise, the attacker may bypass the IDS by intentionally creating negative events.

In order to model the patterns among multiple events, we use variables to help specify timed conditions. A variable is assigned an event attribute value from one node and then used in a timed condition associated with another node. We also use ε as a variable for abstract events. A timed condition is formally defined as follows.

DEFINITION 6.1 A *timed condition* on a system view (*EvtSch, PredSet*) is a Boolean formula with atoms being either (1) comparisons between constants, variables, and event attribute names in *EvtSch*, or (2) of the form

- $p[\varepsilon.begin\_time](a_1, \ldots, a_k)$,

- $p[\varepsilon.end\_time](a_1, \ldots, a_k)$,

- $(\exists t \in [\varepsilon.begin\_time, \varepsilon.end\_time])p[t](a_1, \ldots, a_k)$, or

- $(\forall t \in [\varepsilon.begin\_time, \varepsilon.end\_time])p[t](a_1, \ldots, a_k)$,

where p is a dynamic predicate name in *PredSet* and $a_1, \ldots, a_k$ are constants, variables, or event attribute names in *EvtSch*. A timed condition evaluates to True or False when the variables are replaced with constants and ε with an event.

We are now ready to formally define the concept of a misuse signature.

DEFINITION 6.2 Consider a set of system view instances $S = \{(EvtSch_1, PredSet_1), \ldots, (EvtSch_k, PredSet_k)\}$. A *misuse signature* (or *signature*) on S is a 7-tuple $(N, E, SysView, Label, Assignment, TimedCondition, PositiveNodes)$, where

(1) (N, E) is a directed graph,

(2) *SysView* is a mapping that maps each node n in N to a system view instance in S,

(3) *Label* is a mapping that maps each arc in E to a qualitative temporal relationship between two events,

(4) *Assignment* is a mapping that maps each node n in N to a set of assignments of event attributes in the system view $SysView(n)$ to variables (denoted as *variable := attribute_name*) such that each variable appears in exactly one assignment in the signature,

(5) *TimedCondition* is a mapping that maps each n in N to a timed condition on $SysView(n)$ such that all variables in the timed condition appear in some assignments specified by (4), and

(6) *PositiveNodes* $\neq \emptyset$ is a subset of N.

A misuse signature is an event pattern that represents an intrusive activity over a set of systems represented by the system view instances. The pattern is described by a set of events and the constraints that these events must satisfy. Given a signature $(N, E, SysView, Label, Assignment, TimedCondition, PositiveNodes)$, the set of nodes N represents the set of events involved in the pattern, the edges and the labels associated with the edges, which are specified by the mappings E and *Label*, encode the qualitative temporal relationships between these events, the mapping *TimedCondition* specifies the conditions that each event must satisfy, and the mapping *Assignment* determines attributes that are used in some timed conditions. The set of nodes *PositiveNodes* represents the positive events necessary to constitute an attack, while the set of nodes $(N - PositiveNodes)$ represents the negative events that contribute information to filter out false alarms.

Note that we use the qualitative temporal relationships between events to help specify misuse signatures. However, in order to represent quantitative temporal relationships between events, we will have to assign timestamps to variables and specify them in timed conditions. For example, if we require that two events e_1 and e_2 start within 10 seconds, we can assign $e_1.begin\_time$ to a variable t and then specify e_2's timed condition as $|t - e_2.begin\_time| < 10$ (assuming that the time is measured in second).

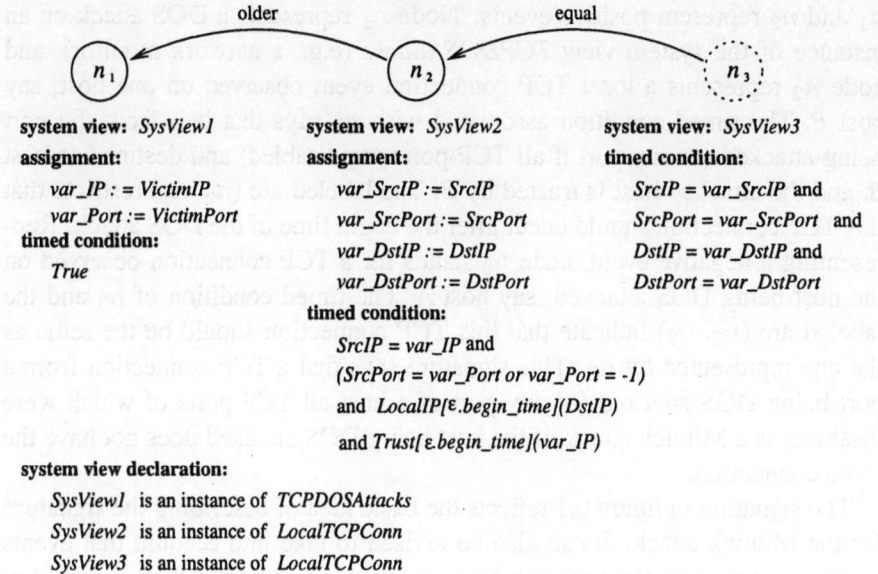

Figure 6.1. The signature for the Mitnick attack

To have a better illustration, we pictorially represent a misuse signature as a labeled graph. Given a signature *Sig* = (*N, E, SysView, Label, Assignment, TimedCondition, PositiveNodes*), the components *N* and *E* are represented by a directed graph, where the nodes in *PositiveNodes* have solid boundary and the other nodes have dotted boundary, the components *SysView, Assignment* and *TimedCondition* are represented by a system view, a set of assignments and a timed condition associated with each node, the component *Label* is represented by a label associated with each arc, and the system view instances underlying the signature are given by a list of declarations of system view instances. An example of misuse signatures is shown as follows.

EXAMPLE 6.1 This example shows a signature of the aforementioned Mitnick attack. It's worth noting that though the original attack involves a SYN flooding attack, an attacker can actually use other methods to disable one or all of the TCP ports of host *A* and achieve the same effect. Thus, the signature for the Mitnick attack should use something more abstract than SYN flooding attack.

Figure 6.1 shows a generic version of the signature for the Mitnick attack. The signature involves three system view instances: an instance of the system view *TCPDOSAttacks* and two instances of *LocalTCPConn*. (The system views *TCPDOSAttacks* and *LocalTCPConn* have been described in example 3.1.) This signature defines a generic pattern for the Mitnick attack. Node

n_1 and n_2 represent positive events. Node n_1 represents a DOS attack on an instance of the system view *TCPDOSAttacks* (e.g., a network monitor), and node n_2 represents a local TCP connection event observed on one host, say host *B*. The timed condition associated with n_2 says that it is from the port being attacked (or any port if all TCP ports are disabled) and destined to host *B*, and the attacked host is trusted by *B*. The labeled arc (n_2, n_1) restricts that this TCP connection should occur after the begin time of the DOS attack. Representing a negative event, node n_3 stands for a TCP connection observed on the host being DOS attacked, say host *A*. The timed condition of n_3 and the labeled arc (n_3, n_2) indicate that this TCP connection should be the same as the one represented by n_2. This signature says that a TCP connection from a port being DOS attacked (or any port of a host all TCP ports of which were disabled) is a Mitnick attack, if the host being DOS attacked does not have the same connection.

The signature in figure 6.1 reflects the basic idea of describing the signature for the Mitnick attack. It can also be revised to take into account that events n_1 and n_2 are often close to each other in time (in addition to that n_2 is older than n_1). Such a signature would be easier to execute, since we do not have to consider a DOS attack and a TCP connection if they are far from each other in time.

Now we clarify the semantics of a misuse signature by formally defining what it matches.

DEFINITION 6.3 Let *Sig* = (*N, E, SysView, Label, Assignment, TimedCondition, PositiveNodes*) be a signature on the set of system view instances *S* = {(*EvtSch$_1$, PredSet$_1$*), ..., (*EvtSch$_k$, PredSet$_k$*)}, and for each $1 \leq i \leq k$, let $\mathcal{H}_i = \{e_{i,1}, \ldots, e_{i,m_i}\}$ be an event history on the system view (*EvtSch$_i$, PredSet$_i$*). For a subset N_s of *N*, a mapping $\pi : N_s \rightarrow \{e_{1,1}, \ldots, e_{1,m_1}, e_{2,1}, \ldots, e_{2,m_2}, \ldots, e_{k,1}, \ldots, e_{k,m_k}\}$ is said to be a *match* of N_s on $\mathcal{H}_1, \ldots, \mathcal{H}_k$ if the following conditions are satisfied:

(1) for each node n in N_s, $\pi(n) = e$ is an event on the system view associated with n and event attribute values of e are assigned to variables according to the assignments associated with n,

(2) for each arc (n_1, n_2) in *E* such that n_1 and n_2 are in N_s, if $\pi(n_1) = e_i$ and $\pi(n_2) = e_j$ and (n_1, n_2) is mapped to a qualitative temporal relationship $\cdot R \cdot$ by the mapping *Label*, then $e_i \cdot R \cdot e_j$, and

(3) for each node n in N_s with a timed condition, if $\pi(n) = e$, then the timed condition is True with ε replaced with e and the variables with the values assigned in (1).

Event#	VictimIP	VictimPort
e_{11}	www.victim.com	80
e_{12}	www.victim.com	80
e_{13}	flooded.victim.com	513

(a) Events generated by the network monitor

Event#	SrcIP	SrcPort	DstIP	DstPort
e_{21}	one.victim.com	8765	target.victim.com	23
e_{22}	host.another.com	4000	target.victim.com	7
e_{23}	flooded.victim.com	513	target.victim.com	514

(b) Local TCP events on the host target.victim.com

Event#	SrcIP	SrcPort	DstIP	DstPort	Protocol
e_{31}	one.victim.com	8789	flooded.victim.com	23	
e_{32}	host.another.com	7863	flooded.victim.com	21	
e_{33}	flooded.victim.com	20	host.another.com	7864	

(c) Local TCP events on the host flooded.victim.com

Figure 6.2. Events on the system views

A match π of *PositiveNodes* on $\mathcal{H}_1, \ldots, \mathcal{H}_k$ is said to be a *match* of *Sig* if (1) $N = PositiveNodes$, or (2) $N \neq PositiveNodes$ and there does not exist a match π' of N such that π and π' are the same for nodes in *PositiveNodes*.

EXAMPLE 6.2 Suppose the network monitor in example 6.1 has detected the DOS attacks shown in figure 6.2(a). (For simplicity, all timestamps are omitted.) Also, suppose the hosts *target.victim.com* and *flooded.victim.com* have TCP connection events shown in figure 6.2(b) and 6.2(c), and *target.victim.com* trusts *flooded.victim.com* (i.e., for all time point t, $Trust[t](flooded.victim.com)$ = True). Suppose event e_{23} is older than event e_{13} (i.e., $e_{13}.begin\_time <$ $e_{23}.begin\_time$). Then e_{13} and e_{23} satisfy all the conditions specified for nodes n_1 and n_2. In addition, there does not exist any event on the host *flooded.victim.com* that satisfies the conditions for node n_3 along with e_{13} and e_{23}. Thus, events e_{13} and e_{23} constitute a match of the signature. In other words, an instance of the Mitnick attack is detected.

Nodes in a signature represent (abstract) events on system views; therefore, in the following discussion, we will use nodes and events interchangeably.

2.   Defining System Views Using Signatures: A Hierarchical Model

In this section, we further extend the abstraction-based misuse detection model to define system views on the basis of signatures. The system view defined in this way presents an interface for the information extracted (or aggregated) from the events that match the corresponding signatures, and thus provides a more concise view of what has happened or is happening in the systems. Indeed, this approach allows signatures to be specified hierarchically since signatures are defined on the basis of system views.

There are several benefits of this extension. First, it reduces the complexity of specifying signatures. Having the ability to hierarchically define signatures allows a user to decompose a complex attack into logical components and resolve them separately, thus allows a divide and conquer strategy in the signature specification process. Second, this approach allows scalable implementations. For example, the hierarchically defined signatures can be easily applied to a hierarchical distributed IDS such that a lower-level IDS sends the information condensed through the lower-level signature and system view to a higher-level IDS. Since the events on derived system views convey only the selected and aggregated information, they are usually much less than the original events. Therefore, with a carefully designed system and signatures, we can avoid having intractably large amount of data even in a very large system.

Intuitively, we derive the information on a system view (which is called the *derived system view*) from the matches of a signature in two steps. Step 1: for each combination of events that match the signature, we take the necessary information from them by assigning their attribute values to the variables (which is indicated by the assignments). In other words, the selected attribute values of an event are assigned to the variables if the event corresponds to a positive node in a match. As a result, we can consider that each signature has a relation whose attributes are the variables that appear in the assignments associated with positive nodes, and each tuple in this relation consists of the attribute values assigned to the variables in a match. We call the schema of such a relation the *matched view* and the information provided through the matched view the *match history* of the signature. For example, the signature of the Mitnick attack (shown in figure 6.1) has a matched view whose schema is (var_IP, var_Port, var_SrcIP, $var\_SrcPort$, var_DstIP, $var\_DstPort$), and the tuples in this view will be the corresponding IP addresses and port numbers involved in Mitnick attacks.

Step 2: we apply a function to process the matched history. The function takes the tuples on the matched view as input and outputs events on the derived system view. In particular, we identify a special class of functions that can be executed in real time. That is, the function can be applied to a match of the signature once it is detected. The events (on the derived system view) generated this way correspond to the compound events represented by the detection of signatures. For simplicity, we choose a subset of the dynamic predicates in the underlying system views as the predicate set in the new one. An easy extension could be to use logical combinations of the underlying dynamic predicates in the derived system view.

In the following, we first formally define the notions of matched view and matched history, then formalize the derivation of system views from signatures as *view definition*.

DEFINITION 6.4 Let *Sig* = (*N, E, SysView, Label, Assignment, TimedCondition, PositiveNodes*) be a signature on a set of system view instances $S = \{(EvtSch_1, PredSet_1), \ldots, (EvtSch_k, PredSet_k)\}$. The *matched view* of *Sig* derived from S, denoted (V), is a relation schema that consists of all the variables appearing in the assignments associated with the nodes in *PositiveNodes*. Moreover, for each i, $1 \leq i \leq k$, let $\mathcal{H}_i$ be an event history on $(EvtSch_i, PredSet_i)$. The *matched history* of *Sig* derived from $\mathcal{H}_1, \ldots, \mathcal{H}_k$ is a relation on (V) that consists of one tuple t for each match of *Sig* on $\mathcal{H}_1, \ldots, \mathcal{H}_k$ and the attribute values of t are the values assigned to the variables in the match.

DEFINITION 6.5 Given a set S of system view instances, a *view definition* on S is a 4-tuple (*Sig, EvtSch, PredSet, f*), where

(1) *Sig* is a signature on S;

(2) *EvtSch* is a set of event attribute names, each with an associated domain of values;

(3) *PredSet* is a subset of all the dynamic predicates appearing in S;

(4) f is a function that takes tuples of the matched view of *Sig* and outputs tuples on *EvtSch* with interval-based timestamps.

The system view (*EvtSch, PredSet*) is called the system view derived by the view definition, or simply *derived system view*.

A view definition (*Sig, EvtSch, PredSet, f*) derives a system view on the basis of the signature *Sig*. *EvtSch* specifies the event schema of the derived system view, *PredSet* indicates the dynamic predicates inherited from the underlying system views, and f describes how the matches of *Sig* are transformed into events on *EvtSch*.

A critical component of a view definition is the function f. A special class of function f is to post-process the matches of the signature and generate a compound event for each match. Typically, such a function f takes a match of *Sig*, selects some attributes of interest, and presents them through the derived system view. Information extracted this way may be used for high-level attack correlation or intrusion response. For simplicity, we use an SQL query of the form *SELECT-FROM-WHERE*, which is targeted to a single instance of the matched view, to specify such a function. Note that using a simplified SQL query does not imply that we have to use a SQL engine or DBMS; it can be simply executed by taking a match once it is detected, evaluating the condition in the *WHERE* clause and renaming the variables of interest. Such queries can be executed at the time when the matches of the signatures are detected, and thus support real-time processing of the detection results.

However, SQL queries (even in unrestricted forms) are not expressive enough; some event processing semantics cannot be expressed using such queries. For example, aggregation in terms of sliding time window cannot be expressed using SQL. An alternative approach is to use rule-based languages to describe the function f. Rule-based languages are more expressive than *SELECT-FROM-WHERE* SQL statements; however, they cannot cover all possible event processing semantics, either. For example, both P-BEST [Lindqvist and Porras, 1999] and RUSSEL [Mounji, 1997, Mounji et al., 1995] depend on external functions to extend their expressiveness. In addition, unlike *SELECT-FROM-WHERE* SQL statements, which can be executed by evaluating conditions and choosing/renaming attributes, rule-based languages require additional mechanisms to execute the rules.

Additional work is required to clarify what representation mechanisms are needed to specify the function f of a view definition. However, since our focus in this dissertation is the framework of signature specification and event abstraction, we consider f as a customizable blackbox and use *SELECT-FROM (V)-WHERE* for some special cases.

EXAMPLE 6.3 Suppose we modify the signature *Mitnick* in figure 6.1 by associating assignments *var_tm1 := begin_time* and *var_tm2 := end_time* with nodes n_1 and n_2, respectively. We can then have the following view definition *MitnickAttacks= (Mitnick', {Attack, VictimHost, VictimPort, Trusted-Host}, {Trust[t](var_host)})*, where *Mitnick'* is the revised signature and *Query* is defined by the following SQL statement.

> SELECT 'Mitnick' AS Attack, var_DstIP AS VictimHost,
>   var_DstPort AS VictimPort, var_SrcIP AS TrustedHost,
>   var_tm1 AS begin_time, var_tm2 AS end_time
> FROM (V)

The system view derived by *MitnickAttacks* is (*{Attack, VictimHost, Victim-Port, TrustedHost}, {Trust[t](var_host)}*).

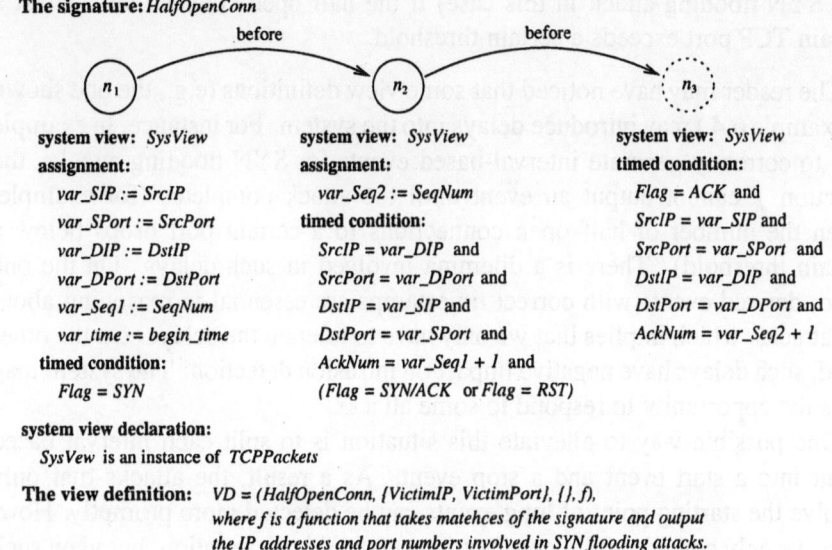

The signature: *HalfOpenConn*

system view: *SysView*	**system view:** *SysView*
assignment:	**assignment:**
$var\_SIP := SrcIP$	$var\_Seq2 := SeqNum$
$var\_SPort := SrcPort$	**timed condition:**
$var\_DIP := DstIP$	$SrcIP = var\_DIP$ and
$var\_DPort := DstPort$	$SrcPort = var\_DPort$ and
$var\_Seq1 := SeqNum$	$DstIP = var\_SIP$ and
$var\_time := begin\_time$	$DstPort = var\_SPort$ and
timed condition:	$AckNum = var\_Seq1 + 1$ and
$Flag = SYN$	$(Flag = SYN/ACK$ or $Flag = RST)$

system view: *SysView*
timed condition:
$Flag = ACK$ and
$SrcIP = var\_SIP$ and
$SrcPort = var\_SPort$ and
$DstIP = var\_DIP$ and
$DstPort = var\_DPort$ and
$AckNum = var\_Seq2 + 1$

system view declaration:

SysVew is an instance of *TCPPackets*

The view definition: $VD = (HalfOpenConn, \{VictimIP, VictimPort\}, \{\}, f)$,
where *f* is a function that takes matehces of the signature and output
the IP addresses and port numbers involved in SYN flooding attacks.

Figure 6.3. The view definition for deriving SYN flooding events from TCP packets

EXAMPLE 6.4 We consider a view definition that aggregates TCP/IP packet events into compound events representing SYN flooding attacks on the system view *TCPDOSAttacks* (discussed in example 3.1). Suppose the TCP/IP packet information is provided through a system view *TCPPacket* = (*EvtSch*, $\emptyset$), where *EvtSch* = {*SrcIP, SrcPort, DstIP, DstPort, SeqNum, AckNum, Flag*}. These attributes represent the source address, the source port, the destination address, the destination port, the sequence number, the acknowledge number and the flag associated with each packet. The domain of *Flag* is the set of valid TCP flags, including *SYN, SYN/ACK, ACK, RST*, etc. The domains of other attributes are clear from the names. (This system view can be directly generated by tools like tcpdump.)

Figure 6.3 shows the signature *HalfOpenConn* and the view definition *VD* that defines the derived system view on the basis of *HalfOpenConn*. Node n_1 represents a SYN packet that initiates a TCP connection, and node n_2 represents a SYN/ACK packet or a RESET packet that responds to the SYN packet. Both node n_1 and n_2 represent positive events. The negative node n_3 represents an ACK packet that finalize a TCP three-way handshake. Thus, a match of *HalfOpenConn* indicates either a half open connection or a connection reset during the TCP three-way handshake. The component *f* is a function (or procedure) that takes the matches of *HalfOpenConn* as input and output the IP address, TCP port and the timestamp of SYN flooding attacks. One way to implement *f* is to use a sliding time window and report a TCPDOSAttack (which is a SYN flooding attack in this case) if the half open connections against a certain TCP port exceeds a certain threshold.

The reader may have noticed that some view definitions (e.g., the one shown in example 6.4) may introduce delays into the system. For instance, in example 6.4, to correctly generate interval-based events for SYN flooding attacks, the function f cannot output an event until the attack completes (for example, when the number of half open connections to a certain port drops below a certain threshold). There is a dilemma involved in such delays. On the one hand, derived events with correct timestamps are essential in reasoning about the attacks, which implies that we may have to tolerate the delays. On the other hand, such delays have negative impact on intrusion detection: The system may miss the opportunity to respond to some attacks.

One possible way to alleviate this situation is to split each interval based event into a start event and a stop event. As a result, the attacks that only involve the starting point of long events can be detected more promptly. However, we only consider fully generated events in this dissertation, but view such an approach as a possible future work.

We call the information that a derived system view extracts or aggregates from the underlying event histories a derived event history, which is formally defined as follows.

DEFINITION 6.6 Let $VD = (Sig, EvtSch, PredSet, f)$ be a view definition on a set of system view instances $S = \{(EvtSch_1, PredSet_1), \ldots, (EvtSch_k, PredSet_k)\}$ and for $1 \leq i \leq k$, let $\mathcal{H}_i$ be an event history on $(EvtSch_i, PredSet_i)$. Then the *event history on $(EvtSch, PredSet)$ derived from* $\mathcal{H}_1, \ldots, \mathcal{H}_k$ consists of

(1) a set of events that f outputs by taking as input the matched history of *Sig* derived from $\mathcal{H}_1, \ldots, \mathcal{H}_k$, and

(2) the instantiation (in $\mathcal{H}_1, \ldots, \mathcal{H}_k$) of the dynamic predicate names in *Pred-Set*.

Each event in the derived event history is called a *derived event*.

EXAMPLE 6.5 Consider the view definition shown in example 6.3. Suppose the event histories on the system view instances underlying this view definition are the same as in example 6.2 (see figure 6.2). Then based on the discussion in example 6.2, the events in the derived event history are shown in table 6.1, and *Trust[t](var_host)* evaluates to True if *var_host* is trusted by the victim host at time t.

The introduction of view definition allows a hierarchical organization of system views and signatures. Such a hierarchical model not only provides a framework for attack specification and event abstraction, but also ensures that

Table 6.1. Events in the derived history

Attack	VictimHost	VictimPort	TrustedHost
Mitnick	target.victim.com	514	flooded.victim.com

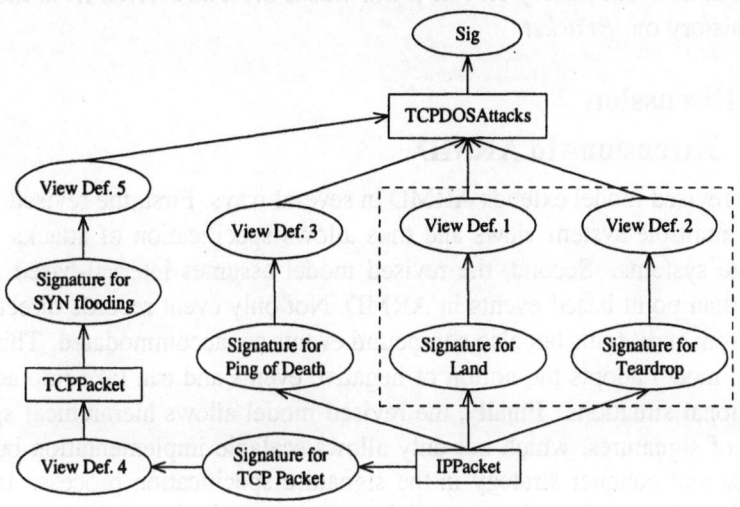

Figure 6.4. A hierarchy of system views and signatures

abstraction becomes a dynamic and on-going process. Figure 6.4 shows a hierarchy of system views, signatures, and view definitions. Notice that such a hierarchy may evolve along time. For example, when we initially specify the system view *TCPDOSAttacks*, we may be only aware of two types of such attacks: *Land* and *Teardrop* (see [Kendall, 1999] for details). Thus, we may derive information on *TCPDOSAttacks* from *IPPacket* using signatures for *Land* and *Teardrop* and the corresponding view definitions, as shown in the dashed box in figure 6.4. Certainly, signatures can be specified on the basis of *TCPDOSAttacks* once it is defined. However, we may later discover other TCP based DOS attacks, e.g., Ping of Death and SYN flooding attacks [Kendall, 1999]. If this happens, we can use signatures and view definitions (e.g., the signatures and view definitions outside of the dashed box in figure 6.4) to derive more events on *TCPDOSAttacks* without changing either the specification of *TCPDOSAttacks* itself or the signatures defined on the basis of it. In other words, we can gradually change the semantics of system views and signatures without changing their specifications. As a result, the signatures specified in our model are generic and can potentially accommodate new attacks.

As illustrated in figure 6.4, an instance of system view may have multiple sources to derive its event history. For example, one event history on *TCPDOSAttacks* may be derived using all the four view definitions below it. To ensure the derived information is meaningful and consistent, we require that an event history on a derived system view must be generated from the same set of event histories on the underlying system views. In our example, all information of an event history on *TCPDOSAttacks* must be derived from the same event history on *IPPacket*.

3. Discussion
3.1 Extensions to ARMD

The revised model extends ARMD in several ways. First, the revised model allows multiple system views and thus allows specification of attacks across multiple systems. Second, the revised model assumes interval-based events rather than point-based events in ARMD. Not only event records directly derived from audit trails but also compound events are accommodated. Third, the revised model adopts the notion of negative events and can take into account exceptional situations. Finally, the revised model allows hierarchical specification of signatures, which not only allows scalable implementation but also a divide and conquer strategy in the signature specification process. Indeed, ARMD can be considered as a special case of the revised model; all the attacks that can be specified by ARMD can be described by the revised model.

3.2 Generic and Specific Signatures

A signature in our model specifies a generic pattern of a certain type of attacks, which is usually independent of any specific systems. This is because signatures are defined on the abstract representations of underlying systems (i.e. system views), and this abstraction usually leads to generic signatures that can accommodate variants of the original attack. However, when the attack is to be detected, the signature has to be mapped to specific systems so that the IDS can reason the events observed on the specific systems according to the signature.

To distinguish the aforementioned two situations, we call a signature a *specific signature* if each system view instance used by the signature is associated with a particular system for the corresponding system view. In contrast, we call a signature a *generic signature* if there is at least one system view instance not associated with any system. For example, the signature shown in figure 6.1 is a generic signature since no system view instance is associated with any system. If we associate the three system view instances to a network monitor M and two hosts A and B, it becomes a specific signature representing the Mitnick attack on these systems. Note that in this dissertation we consider a signature being generic or specific as a system feature and not include it in the formal model.

One generic signature usually corresponds to more than one specific signature, since the attacks modeled by the generic signature may happen against different targets. It is desirable to model attacks as generic signatures. When the attacks are to be detected for particular target systems, the specific signatures can be generated from the generic ones by associating the system view instances with appropriate systems. However, this does not mean that one can only write generic signatures. One can also write a specific signature for a particular system according to the configuration of the system.

3.3 Clock Discrepancy

The model assumes that all the clocks in different systems are well synchronized, which usually is not true in the real systems. The clock discrepancy can certainly affect the detection of attacks. For example, consider a signature that requires two events happen at the same time, it would be difficult to detect such an attack if the two events are from two different systems whose clocks do not agree. Indeed, clock discrepancy will increase both the false positive and the possibility to mistaken attacks for normal activities if time is involved in the misuse signature.

A simple countermeasure is to set up a threshold t as the maximal difference between distributed clocks and handle timestamps in a special way. Specifically, two time points t_1 and t_2 in two different places are considered "equal" if $|t_1 - t_2| < t$, and t_1 is considered "before" t_2 if $t_1 - t < t_2$. A higher threshold will certainly help to tolerate worse clock discrepancy, but it will also result in a higher false alarm rate.

A true solution is to have a distributed time synchronization service that keeps the clock discrepancy between related systems at a tolerable level. This service should be secure so that attackers cannot create clock discrepancy to avoid being detected. Though very interesting, this problem is out of the scope of this dissertation. Nevertheless, the clock discrepancy problem is not unique to our model; if the time relationship between distributed events is intrinsic to an attack, we cannot avoid this problem no matter what model we use.

Chapter 7

DECENTRALIZED DETECTION OF DISTRIBUTED ATTACKS

Research efforts on scalable distributed intrusion detection have been focused on hierarchical IDSs, which organize IDSs into hierarchies and require low-level IDSs send designated information to high-level IDSs. The hierarchies of IDSs are usually developed according to administrative concerns. For example, IDSs for individual hosts are organized under IDSs for departments, while IDSs for departments are organized under an IDS for the entire enterprise. However, there are often mismatches between such organizations of IDSs and detection of distributed attacks. In this chapter, we present an alternative approach to organizing autonomous but cooperative component systems to detect distributed attacks. Our approach is based on the dependency among the distributed events in a signature. Unlike the hierarchical approach, our approach organizes the cooperative IDSs according to the intrinsic relationships between the distributed events involved in attacks, and, as a result, an IDS needs to send a piece of information to another IDS only when the information is essential for detecting the attacks.

1. Serializable Signatures

Not all signatures can be detected efficiently in a distributed way. Before presenting our approach for distributed misuse detection, we first demonstrate a "problematic" signature and then identify the signatures with which we have efficient algorithms.

Consider the signature shown in figure 7.1. Assume that the systems underlying the system view instances *SysView1* and *SysView2* are host 1 and host 2, respectively. Note that the timed condition associated with n_1 needs the variable $x2$ assigned at node n_2, while the timed condition with n_2 requires the variable $x1$ assigned at n_1. Suppose both host 1 and host 2 want to process their events locally. Whenever an event e_1 occurs, host 1 needs to send corre-

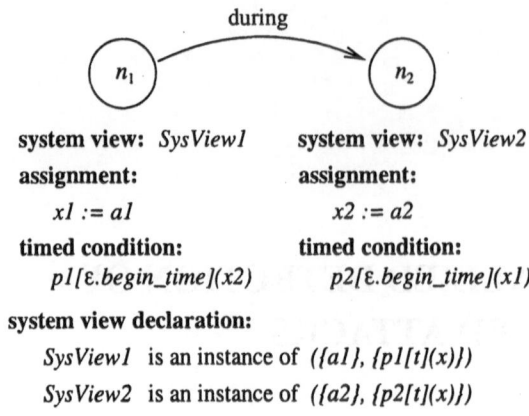

Figure 7.1. A non-serializable signature

sponding information (at least the value of $x1$) to host 2, since the value of $x1$ is needed to evaluate the events represented by n_2. Similarly, all the events that occur on host 2 need to be sent to host 1. In this example, each event requires a message. When there are more nodes that need information from each other, more messages will be required. For such signatures, a distributed approach entails more messages; indeed, a centralized approach is more appropriate.

The nature of this problem is the relationship between different nodes (abstract events) in a signature. We clarify this relationship as follows. We say that a node n *requires* a variable x if x appears in the timed condition associated with n. For any two nodes n and n' in a signature, we say n *directly requires* n' if n requires some variables assigned at n'. Moreover, we say n *requires* n' if n directly requires n' or there exists another node n'' such that n requires n'' and n'' directly requires n'. For example, in figure 7.1 both n_1 requires n_2 and n_2 requires n_1, since n_1 requires the variable $x2$ assigned at n_2 and n_2 requires the variable $x1$ assigned at n_1. As another example, in figure 6.1 n_2 requires n_1, and n_3 requires both n_2 and n_1. Intuitively, node n needs information from node n' through variable assignments if n (directly) requires n'.

Now we identify the signatures that can avoid the above situations by the notion of serializable signature.

DEFINITION 7.1 A signature S is *serializable* if (1) the binary relation *require* on the set of nodes in S is irreflexive, and (2) no positive node requires any negative node.

The signature in figure 6.1 is an example of serializable signatures: the relation *require* on the set of nodes $\{n_1, n_2, n_3\}$ is irreflexive and the only negative node n_3 is not required by any node. However, the signature in figure 7.1 is not serializable, since n_1 and n_2 require each other.

Since the relation *require* is transitive by definition, it is implied that the relation *require* on the set of nodes of a serializable signature is a strict partial order.

Some non-serializable signatures can be transformed into equivalent serializable ones. Consider a variant of the signature in figure 6.1 in which the comparison $SrcIP = var\_IP$ is not placed in the timed condition associated with node n_2 but represented equivalently as $var\_SrcIP = VictimIP$ and placed in the timed condition associated with n_1. Then this signature is not serializable, since node n_1 and n_2 require each other. However, we can always transform it back into the equivalent form shown in figure 6.1. Indeed, for any two nodes that require each other in a non-serializable signature, if one of the problematic variables appears in a conjunctive term of the timed condition that does not involve dynamic predicate, we can always place it into another timed condition as we did above so that the two nodes no longer require each other.

In the rest of this chapter, we will only consider the detection of attacks specified by serializable signatures.

2. Detection Task and Workflow Tree

A signature for a distributed attack is composed of events distributed over multiple systems. When detecting such attacks, communication between different systems is inevitable, since the evidences from different places need to be correlated in some way in order to reason about the attacks. To avoid transmitting all the distributed events to a centralized place for analysis, we let each system process the events that it observes and all the systems that are involved in a signature collaborate to perform the detection.

We consider the nodes in a signature as the basic processing units. An alternative is to treat all or some of the nodes in one system as one unit; however, we will have to process the events for different nodes in one unit differently and thus have a similar result. For the sake of description, we informally call the processing for a node n a *detection task* for n. (We will clarify the semantics of detection task later by a formal definition.) Intuitively, a detection task for node n determines whether an event corresponding to n satisfies the conditions related to n.

The detection tasks in a signature are not isolated due to the relationships between the nodes. In particular, the detection task for node n needs the information from the detection task for node n' if n requires n'. For example, consider the signature shown in figure 6.1. Given only the events on *SysView2*, the detection task for node n_2 will not be able to determine whether such an event satisfies the condition for n_2 without the variable var_IP assigned at node n_1. Therefore, we need to coordinate the detection tasks in a signature in order to successfully perform the intrusion detection.

Several issues are worth considering. First, the relation *require* on the set of nodes in the signature should be reflected in the coordination. As we discussed earlier, the relation *require* imposes that the detection task for node n' should give information to the detection task for n if n requires n'. Second, positive events represent possible attacks; to ensure the security of the system, positive events should be processed as soon as possible. Third, since the goal is to determine whether a set of events constitutes an attack, the results of all the detection tasks should finally be correlated together.

We use *workflow tree* to represent the coordination of the detection tasks in a signature. The nodes in a workflow tree consists of all the nodes in the signature, and an edge from one node to the other indicates that the detection task for the latter node should send information (variable values and timestamps) to the task for the former one. The workflow tree is formally defined as follows.

DEFINITION 7.2 A *workflow tree* for a serializable signature *Sig* is a tree whose nodes are all the nodes in *Sig* and whose edges satisfy the following conditions: (1) given two nodes n_1 and n_2 in *Sig*, n_2 is a descendant of n_1 if n_1 requires n_2, and (2) there exists a subtree that contains all and only the positive nodes in *Sig*.

Condition 1 says that the detection task for node n_1 (directly or indirectly) receives information from the detection task for node n_2 if n_1 requires n_2; condition 2 says that the detection tasks for positive events must be performed before any the detection tasks for any negative event. Moreover, the tree structure ensures that all the results of the detection tasks will finally be correlated together. Figure 7.2(a) shows a workflow tree for the signature in figure 6.1.

In a workflow tree, the root of the subtree that contains all and only the detection tasks for the positive nodes is called the *positive root*, and the root of the entire tree, if a negative node, is called the *workflow tree, negative root*. For example, in figure 7.2(a), node n_2 is the positive root while node n_3 is the negative root.

Note that a workflow tree specifies the coordination of the detection tasks involved in an attack; it does not specify the order of involved events. One node being a child of another does not imply that the former node must happen before the latter one.

Another issue is the arrangement of signature, negative nodes in workflow trees. In our current approach, all signature, positive nodes are arranged in a subtree, and no negative node can appear under positive nodes. One may think that having negative nodes between or under positive nodes can improve the performance. It is worth pointing out that negative events are possibly observable events, not filtering conditions. It is true that if we already observed some

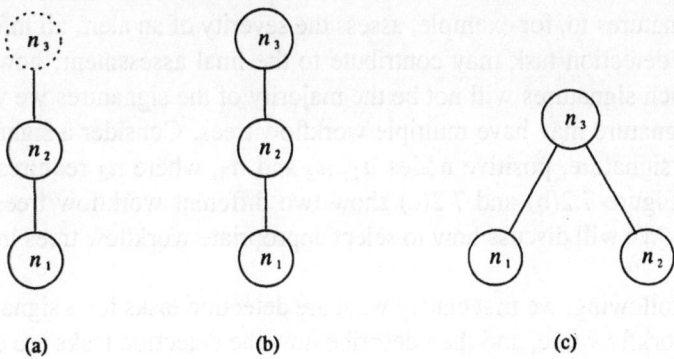

Figure 7.2. Examples of workflow trees

negative events, we may be able to invalidate some positive events without going through all positive nodes. However, such an arrangement also introduces
difficult situations if we do not observe the corresponding negative events. In
this case, we have to send the corresponding positive information to the rest
of positive nodes, and two situations may follow. On the one hand, if we do
not later discover the rest of positive events, then sending positive information through negative detection tasks already costs more. On the other hand,
if we do find all positive events involved in a possible attack, we still need to
check with the previously visited negative events, since some negative events
may be observed after the previous check. Thus, the aforementioned approach
does not always result in better performance than workflow tree. Further considering the simplicity of workflow tree, we choose our current approach to
coordinate the detection tasks.

There are other alternative ways to represent the coordination of detection
tasks. For example, we may represent the coordination of detection tasks in
one signature as a directed acyclic graph with one sink, where the nodes are
the detection tasks, and an edge from one detection task to another represents
that the former detection task should send information to the latter one. An
important distinction between this alternative representation and the workflow
tree is that in the former representation, each detection task may send messages
to multiple detection tasks, while in the workflow tree, each detection task
sends information to at most one detection task, and the information required
by more than one detection task is first sent to one task and then forwarded to
the others. Since most of the events in normal situations are normal, most of
the information sent by a detection task is expected not related to an attack.
Using the workflow tree can not only simplify the model, but also reduce the
number of messages when most of the messages are determined useless and not

forwarded to other detection tasks. In some special cases where we would like to use signatures to, for example, assess the severity of an alert, all information sent by a detection task may contribute to the final assessment; however, we believe such signatures will not be the majority of the signatures we will use.

One signature may have multiple workflow trees. Consider a signature that has three signature, positive nodes n_1, n_2 and n_3, where n_3 requires both n_1 and n_2. Figure 7.2(b) and 7.2(c) show two different workflow trees for this signature. We will discuss how to select appropriate workflow trees in the next section.

In the following, we first clarify what are detection tasks for a signature with a given workflow tree, and then describe how the detection tasks are executed.

DEFINITION 7.3 Given a serializable signature *Sig* = (*N, E, SysView, Label, Assignment, TimedCondition, PositiveNodes*) and a workflow tree *T* for *Sig*, the *detection task* for each *n* in *N* is a 11-tuple (*n, sysview, assign, cond, p, PM, C, CPM, type, isRoot, negativeRoot*), where

- *sysview* = *SysView(n)*,

- *assign* = *Assignment(n)* $\cup\{begin\_time_n := begin\_time, end\_time_n := end\_time\}$,

- *cond* is the conjunction of *TimedCondition(n)* and the qualitative temporal relationships (represented by *E* and *Label*) between *n* and *n*'s descendants in *T*,

- *p* is the parent node of *n* in *T* if *n* is not the root, or *p* is the positive root if *n* is the negative root,

- *PM* = $\{begin\_time_{n'}, end\_time_{n'} \mid n' = n$ or *n*'s descendants$\} \cup \{$the variables assigned at *n* and *n*'s descendants and required by *n*'s ancestors$\}$,

- *C* is the set of child nodes of *n* in *T* if *n* is not a leaf, and *C* contains the negative root node if *n* is the positive root node but not the root of the whole workflow tree,

- *CPM* is a mapping from *C* to sets of variables such that for each $c \in C$, *CPM(c)* is the *PM* component of the detection task for *c*,

- *type* = *positive* if $n \in PositiveNodes$, and *type* = *negative* otherwise, and

- *isRoot* = *True* if *n* is the root of *T* or the subtree of *T* that consists of all the nodes in *PositiveNodes*, and *isRoot* = *False* otherwise, and

- if *n* is the positive root and *T* has negative nodes, *negativeRoot* is the root of *T*; otherwise, *negativeRoot* is *NULL* (invalid).

The formal definition of detection task specifies all the information required for the processing of each event in a signature as well as how this information is derived from the signature and the corresponding workflow tree. The component n identifies the event in the original signature; the component *sysview* indicates the system view instance from which the detection task gets event and state information about the monitored system; the component *cond* specifies the condition that should be tested against each event on *sysview*; the component *assign* includes all the assignments of event attributes to variables that should be performed if an event on *sysview* satisfies *cond*; the component p identifies the detection task (i.e., the *parent detection task*) to which this detection task should send detection related messages; the component *PM* specifies the schema of the messages to be sent to the parent detection task; the component C identifies all the detection tasks (i.e., the *child detection tasks*) from which this detection task is going to receive detection related messages; similar to *PM*, the component *CPM* specifies the schema of the messages to be received from each child detection task; the component *type* indicates whether this detection task corresponds to a positive or a negative event; finally, the component *isRoot* tells if this detection task corresponds to the root of the workflow tree or the subtree consisting of all the positive nodes.

Note that timestamp information can be implicitly represented in signatures, while in detection tasks, we explicitly represent the processing of timestamp information by timestamp variables (e.g., $begin\_time_n$ and end_time_n). This is because signatures are provided by human users; thus, using qualitative temporal relationships can usually make this job easier. However, detection tasks are developed for programs; hence, representing the timestamp information explicitly is required.

Let us see an example before we discuss the execution of detection tasks.

EXAMPLE 7.1 Consider the signature for the Mitnick attack in figure 6.1. The detection task for n_1 is $DT_1 = (n_1, SysView1, assign_1, cond_1, n_2, PM_1, \emptyset, NULL, positive, False, NULL)$, where

- $assign_1 = \{var\_IP := VictimIP, var\_Port := VictimPort, begin\_time_{n_1} := begin\_time, end\_time_{n_1} := end\_time\}$,

- $cond_1$ is *True*, and

- $PM_1 = \{begin\_time_{n_1}, end\_time_{n_1}, var\_IP, var\_Port\}$.

This detection task says that it takes events on *SysView1*, which is an instance of *TCPDOSAttacks*, and for each event that satisfies $cond_1$, it makes the assignments in $assign_1$ and sends the assigned values to the detection task for n_2 as a tuple on PM_1.

The detection task for n_2 is $DT_2 = (n_2, SysView2, assign_2, cond_2, n_3, PM_2, C_2, CPM_2, positive, True, n_3)$, where

- $assign_2 = \{var\_SrcIP := SrcIP, var\_SrcPort := SrcPort, var\_DstIP := DstIP,$
  $var\_DstPort := DstPort, begin\_time_{n_2} := begin\_time,$
  $end\_time_{n_2} := end\_time\},$

- $cond_2$ is $((begin\_time > begin\_time_{n_1})$ and $(SrcIP = var\_IP)$ and $(Src-Port = var\_Port)$ and $LocalIP[\varepsilon.begin\_time](DstIP)$ and $Trust[\varepsilon.begin\_time](var\_IP)),$

- $PM_2 = \{var\_SrcIP, var\_SrcPort, var\_DstIP, var\_DstPort, begin\_time_{n_1},$
  $end\_time_{n_1}, begin\_time_{n_2}, end\_time_{n_2}\},$

- $C = \{n_1, n_3\}$, and

- $CPM_2(n_1) = PM_1, CPM_2(n_3) = PM_3.$

This detection task says that it takes events on *SysView2*, which is an instance of *LocalTCPConn*, and receives tuples on PM_1 and PM_3 from the detection tasks for n_1 and n_3, respectively. For each event and the variables that satisfy $cond_2$, it makes the assignments in $assign_2$ and sends the assigned values to the detection task for n_3 as a tuple on PM_2. Note that n_2 is the positive root in the workflow tree. As we will see later, it processes the information from the detection task for the negative root n_3 in a different way.

The detection task for n_3 is $DT_3 = (n_3, SysView3, assign_3, cond_3, n_2, PM_3, C_3, CPM_3, negative, True, NULL)$, where

- $assign_3 = \{begin\_time_{n_3} := begin\_time, end\_time_{n_3} := end\_time\},$

- $cond_3$ is $((begin\_time = begin\_time_{n_2})$ and $(end\_time = end\_time_{n_2})$
  and $(SrcIP = var\_SrcIP)$ and $(SrcPort = var\_SrcPort)$ and
  $(DstIP = var\_DstIP)$ and $(DstPort = var\_DstPort)),$

- $PM_3 = \{begin\_time_{n_1}, end\_time_{n_1}, begin\_time_{n_2}, end\_time_{n_2},$
  $begin\_time_{n_3}, end\_time_{n_3}\},$

- $C = \{n_2\}$, and

- $CPM_3(n_2) = PM_2.$

This detection task says that it takes events on *SysView3*, which is also an instance of *LocalTCPConn*, and receives tuples on PM_2 from its child detection task identified by n_2. For each event and the assigned variable values that satisfy $cond_3$, it makes the assignments in $assign_3$ and sends the assigned values to the detection task for n_2 as a tuple on PM_3 (since n_2 is the positive root in the workflow tree). Here we assume that each event from a particular system is uniquely identified by its timestamp. Note that node n_3 represents a negative event, and a satisfaction of $cond_3$ means that counter evidence is found for a previously discovered match of the signature. Thus, the detection task DT_2 can use the transmitted variable values to mark the match as a false alarm.

Algorithm *DetectionTask*

Input: (1) A detectiontask $DT =$
$$(n, sysview, assign, cond, p, PM, C, CPM, type, isRoot),$$

(2) events on *sysview*, events from the detection tasks for the nodes in C,
and events from the detection task for the negative root node if n is
the positive root.

Output: (1) partial match events sent to the parent task if $p \neq NULL$, and

(2) all the matches of the signature if n is the positive root.

Method:

Let h be an empty relation whose schema is $H = \{begin\_time, end\_time\} \cup$
$\{$all the attributes of *sysview* that appear in *cond* or *assign*$\}$. For each
$c \in C$, let pmt_c be an empty relation whose schema is $CPM(c)$. If n
is the positive root, let m be an empty relation whose schema is PM.

1. **for** each event e **do**
2.   Let $PMT := \emptyset$.
3.   **if** e is an event on *sysview* **then**
4.   Let $PMT := \Pi_{PM}(\rho_{(v:=a) \in assign}(a \rightarrow v, \sigma_{cond}(e \bowtie (\bowtie_{c \in C} pmt_c)))).$
5.   **if** $C \neq \emptyset$ **then**
6.   Let $h := h \cup \Pi_H(e)$.
7.   **if** e is from a child detection task for $c \in C$ **then**
8.   Let $PMT :=$
         $\Pi_{PM}(\rho_{(v:=a) \in assign}(a \rightarrow v, \sigma_{cond}(e \bowtie h \bowtie (\bowtie_{c' \in C \wedge c' \neq c} pmt_{c'})))).$
9.   Let $pmt_c := pmt_c \cup \Pi_{CPM(c)}(e)$.
10.   **if** *type=positive* and *isRoot=True* and e is from the negative root **then**
11.   Let $m := m - \Pi_{PM}(e \bowtie m)$.
12.   **if** $PMT \neq \emptyset$ **then**
13.   **if** $p \neq NULL$ **then**
14.   Send each tuple in PMT to the detection task for p as an event.
15.   **if** *type = positive* and *isRoot = True* **then**
16.   Let $m := m \cup PMT$.

end

Figure 7.3. The algorithm for executing detection task

3. Execution of Detection Tasks

The workflow tree provides a framework for the coordination of the detection tasks. In this subsection, we further explain how each detection task is performed in this framework. We assume that the processing of each event is atomic to ensure the correctness. Allowing concurrent processing of multiple events is interesting and may improve the performance; however, we do not cover it in this dissertation but consider it as possible future work.

Figure 7.3 shows the algorithm for executing a detection task. In order to have a concise description of the algorithm, we adopted some notations from the relational algebra. (Please refer to any database textbook (e.g. [Ullman and Widom, 1997]) for the semantics of the notations.)

The algorithm uses several relations (tables) to keep events and detection result. The relation h, which we call the *detection task, history table*, keeps the necessary information of the events on the system view instance *sysview*. The attributes of the history table consist of the timestamps and the event attributes that appear in *assign* or the condition *cond*. For example, the detection task DT_1 in example 7.1 has the history table whose attributes consist of *VictimIP*, *VictimPort, begin_time* and *end_time*.

For each child node $c \in C$ of n, the relation pmt_c, which we call the *partial match table for c*, keeps the variable values assigned by the child detection task for c. The attributes of pmt_c include all the variables in $CPM(c)$. For example, for the detection task DT_2 in example 7.1 , the partial match table pmt_{n_1} has attributes $begin\_time_{n_1}$, $end\_time_{n_1}$, var_IP, and var_Port.

If n is the positive root node in the corresponding workflow tree, the detection task then keeps a relation m (called the *matched table*) for the detection result of the signature. In figure 7.3, the attributes of the matched table include all the variables in *PM*. Alternatively, we can use all the timestamp variables in *PM* to identify the matches, assuming that each event is uniquely identified by its timestamp.

Note that it is necessary for a detection task to keep both the event information and the variable values received from its child tasks. The detection task may be able to determine that a previously examined event is involved in an attack after receiving additional information from its child tasks. Similarly, the detection task need to examine the information previously received from the child tasks when a local event occurs. Thus, each detection task needs to maintain both a history table and a partial match table for each child detection task. As an exception, the detection tasks without child tasks do not need to maintain any table.

The execution of the algorithm *DetectionTask* is presented in an event-driven fashion. For the sake of presentation, we also consider the variable values sent by a child detection task as an event whose attributes are the variable names. To distinguish between different events, we call the events on system view instances *raw events* and the events sent by a child detection task *partial match events*.

When the detection task receives a raw event e on the system view *sysview* (line 3), it first checks whether e satisfies *cond* along with some tuples in the partial match tables pmt_c. This is specified by a join of e with the partial match tables pmt_c for all c in C (line 4). The schema of the resulting relation is then changed to PM by a series of renaming operations followed by a projection (line 4). Then selected attribute values of e are saved in the history table h if necessary (lines 5 and 6). Figure 7.4(a) illustrates the processing of raw events.

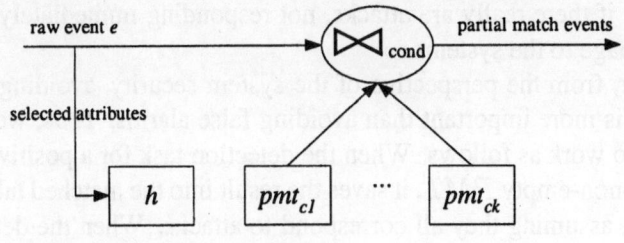

(a) Processing a raw event

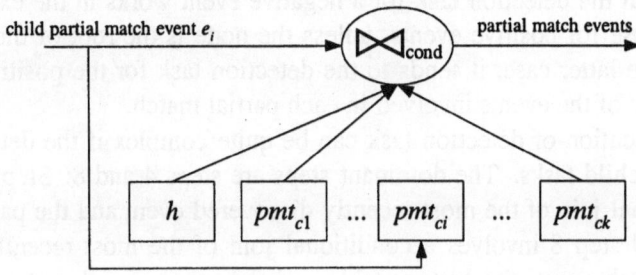

(b) Processing a partial match event

Figure 7.4. Event processing in a detection task

When the detection task receives a partial match event e from a child task c (line 7), it first checks whether this event satisfies *cond* along with the historical events in h and partial match tables for c' other than c. Similarly, this is specified by a join of e with h and all $pmt_{c'}$ for all c' in C other than c (line 8). The schema of the resulting relation is then changed to PM by a series of renaming operations followed by a projection (line 8). Then selected attribute values of e are saved in the partial match table pmt_c as a tuple on $CPM(c)$ (line 9). Figure 7.4(b) illustrates the processing of partial match events.

If the detection task generates new partial match events (i.e., $PMT \neq \emptyset$), it will send all the events to its detection task, parent detection task (denoted by p) if it has one (lines 12 to 14).

As a special case, if the detection task is for a positive root and there are negative nodes in the corresponding workflow tree, the discovery of partial matches (i.e., $PMT \neq \emptyset$) implies possible attacks represented by the signature. This seems to introduce a dilemma. On the one hand, we cannot conclude that an attack really happens if there are negative events in the signature, since we may later discover counter evidences that invalidate these attacks. On the other hand, if there really are attacks, not responding immediately may cause further damage to the systems.

However, from the perspective of the system security, avoiding damage to the system is more important than avoiding false alarms. Thus, we design the algorithm to work as follows. When the detection task for a positive root node discovers a non-empty PMT, it saves the result into the matched table m (lines 15 and 16), assuming they all correspond to attacks. When the detection task for the positive root receives an event e from the detection task for the negative root (i.e., counter evidence of previously detected matches), it then removes all matches that share the same attribute values as e (lines 10 and 11).

Note that the detection task for a negative event works in the exactly same way as those for positive events, unless the node is the root of the workflow tree. In the latter case, it sends to the detection task for the positive root the timestamps of the events involved in each partial match.

The execution of detection task can be quite complex if the detection task has many child tasks. The dominant steps are steps 4 and 8: Step 4 involves a conditional join of the most recently discovered event and the partial match tables, and step 8 involves a conditional join of the most recently received partial match event, the history table and the other partial match tables. A naive implementation of the join operation consists of testing the condition on all combinations of the new event and the tuples in the other tables. Thus, step 4 would involve $\Pi_{c \in C}|pmt_c|$ tests of the condition, and similarly, step 8 would involve $|h| \times \Pi_{c' \in C \wedge c' \neq c}|pmt_c|$ condition tests. Such a method corresponds to exhaustive search, and should be avoided in an implementation.

Two approaches can be used to reduce the execution cost. First, in-memory database query optimization techniques such as in-memory hybrid hash join [DeWitt et al., 1984] and T-Tree [TimesTen Performance Software, 2001] can greatly reduce the cost of the join operation. Indeed, an in-memory database such as TimesTen [TimesTen Performance Software, 2001] can be used in a component IDS to reduce the development cost. Second, some join operations may be materialized to speed-up the event processing. For example, we can pre-compute $\bowtie_{c \in C} pmt_c$ so that when a raw event is discovered, it can be directly joined with the pre-computed table. More research is needed to make the execution of a single detection task efficient; however, we do not address this problem in this dissertation but consider it as future work.

Assume that the communication between detection tasks is *resilient* (i.e., a message inserted into the communication channel will be delivered to the recipient eventually) and the clocks of different IDSs are well synchronized. The correctness of the decomposition and algorithm *DetectionTask* is assured by the following theorem.

THEOREM 7.1 *If all the detection tasks for a signature execute according to the algorithm* DetectionTask, *then they will detect all and only the matches of the signature.*

Proof: Consider a set of detection tasks derived from a signature $Sig = (N, E, SysView, Label, Assignment, TimedCondition, PositiveNodes)$ and a workflow tree T for Sig.

Suppose there is a match of Sig. This implies that for each positive node n in Sig there is an event, denoted e_n, on the system view associated with n such that they together satisfy the three conditions specified in definition 6.3. Consider the detection task DT_l for a leaf node n_l in T. The $cond$ component of DT_l is the timed condition associated with n_l according to definition 7.3. Since the event e_{n_l} satisfies the timed condition associated with n_l (which equals to $cond$) and there is no child detection task, the PMT table in step 4 of the algorithm will contain the values of the variables required by other detection tasks. Assume that the communication between detection tasks does not fail. The variable values in PMT will be sent to the detection task for the parent node of n_l.

Now consider the detection task DT_i for an interior node n_i. Event e_{n_i} will be saved in the history table h at step 6 of the algorithm $DetectionTask$. If DT_i receives the variable values assigned from e_{n_c} for all child nodes n_c of n_i, it will compute a non-empty PMT table in either step 4 (when it receives e_{n_i} after all the variable values) or step 8 (other situations), since e_{n_i} and e_{n_c}'s are part of the match. The table PMT will contain the variable values assigned from e_{n_i} (through the renaming operation) or inherited from the detection tasks for n_i's child nodes. Then in step 14, DT_i will send the variable values to its parent detection task. By induction, the detection task for the positive root node in T will store the timestamps of e_n's. This is to say that all matches of the signature will be detected by the algorithm $DetectionTask$.

For each t in the matched table m, t has timestamp attributes $begin\_time_n$ and end_time_n for each positive node n in Sig, which together identify an event e_n on the system associated with n. For each node n, since $begin\_time_n$ and end_time_n are finally transmitted to the detection task for the positive root, e_n must satisfy the $cond$ component of the corresponding detection task. According to definition 7.3, the $cond$ component of each detection task is the conjunction of the timed condition associated with n and the qualitative temporal relationships between n and n's descendants in T. This has two implications. First, e_n satisfies the timed condition associated with n. Second, for each arc (n_1, n_2) in Sig, either n_1 (when n_1 is closer to the root) or n_2 (when n_2 is closer to the root) satisfying the $cond$ component implies that e_{n_1} and e_{n_2} satisfy the qualitative temporal relationship represented by the labeled arc. This means that there is a match of all the positive nodes.

If $N \neq PositiveNodes$ and there exists a match of all the nodes in Sig, the detection task for the negative root in T will discover this match and sends the timestamp variables to the positive root. Then this match will be removed from m in step 11. This is to say that all the tuples that remain in m long enough (i.e., longer than the time required to process and transmit the negative events) represent matches of the signature Sig. This concludes the proof.   □

Three issues are worth further clarifying about Theorem 7.1. First, Theorem 7.1 ensures the detection of the matches of the signatures, not the attacks themselves. In other words, Theorem 7.1 says that under the aforementioned assumptions, we can detect the attacks as long as the evidences of the attacks are present in the event histories. Second, this theorem does not imply that each alarm raised by the system represents an attack, since an alarm may later be disabled due to the discovery of negative events. Instead, it says that each alarm represents an attack if it stays long enough. The exact threshold to decide whether an alarm is a true positive depends on the network delays and the processing time of the related detection tasks. However, we do not need to identify such a threshold, since it does not contribute to the operation of the system. Third, there is a hidden assumption under the theorem: infinite memory. That is, we never discard any information from the history tables or the partial match tables. However, in reality, we may have to discard some data from these tables due to the memory limitation. As a result, we may miss some stealthy attacks or have false alarms.

4.   Optimization

As we pointed out earlier, one signature may have several workflow trees. Detecting the same signature with different workflow trees may result in different performance, since they may have different storage requirements and different patterns of message transmission between detection tasks. We will discuss how to select a good workflow tree in the next section.

Even with a fixed workflow tree, optimization is still available to improve the performance. Sometimes a detection task can determine that an event on the system view is not involved in an attack even if it needs information from other detection tasks. For example, in the workflow tree in figure 7.2(a), which is a workflow tree for the signature in figure 6.1, the detection task for n_2 can decide that a TCP connection event e is not involved in any attack if the destination IP address does not belong to the host being monitored (i.e., $LocalIP[e.begin\_time](DstIP) = False$). In general, we can transform the $cond$ component of a detection task into the conjunction of two conditions such that one of them involves only the event attributes and constants. We call this part of the $cond$ component a $sieving\ condition$. In the above example, the sieving condition is $LocalIP[e.begin\_time](DstIP)$. The sieving conditions can be evaluated without any information from other detection tasks, and only the events that satisfy the sieving condition need further consideration. Moreover, if we can measure the likelihood that each conjunctive term of *cond* is false, we can check those that have higher likelihood of being false and thus avoid unnecessary evaluations.

Another observation reveals a further optimization opportunity. This can be explained with the above example. In order for an event e on the system view instance *SysView2* to be a part of an attack, it must satisfy $SrcIP = var\_IP$, which is implied by the condition $cond_2$. This means that we can replace var_IP with $SrcIP$ in the predicate $Trust[\varepsilon.begin\_time](var\_IP)$ and still have an equivalent condition. As a result, the sieving condition of the detection task n_2 can be expanded to $(Trust[\varepsilon.begin\_time](Src\_IP)$ *and* $LocalIP[\varepsilon.begin\_time](DstIP))$ and filter out more events than the original one. In general, we can perform an equality analysis through the assignments and the timed conditions in the signature to find out all variables and attributes that are equivalent to each other. Then in the condition component *cond* of each detection task, if a variable is equivalent to an attribute of the system view instance, we can replace the variable with the attribute.

The reader may have noticed that when the size of the history and the partial match tables grow very large, the performance of the algorithm *Detection-Task* may be greatly affected due to the join operations (lines 4 and 7 in figure 7.3). Moreover, the detection task may not be able to grow these tables when memory is limited. A practical solution, which has been used many times in similar contexts (e.g., the token replacement policy in [Kumar, 1995]), is to periodically remove out-of-date tuples from the history and the partial match tables (using certain replacement policy). This can certainly improve the performance; however, in theory the revised algorithm may miss some stealthy attacks, since some evidence could be removed before being correlated with others. More severely, an attacker may intentionally create a large amount of partial matches to launch a denial of service attack against the IDS. To detect such attempts, a statistic (e.g., the size of the table) may have to be associated with each history/partial match table. Nevertheless, this is a problem common to all IDSs that need to keep state about partial detection results (e.g., USTAT [Ilgun et al., 1995]).

The algorithm *DetectionTask* requires that each detection task maintain a history table for the raw events that are possibly involved in attacks. However, one event may be stored in more than one history table if several detection tasks take raw events from the same system view instance. An alternative way to avoid this situation is to maintain one history table for each system view instance. However, this approach is not a silver bullet either. When a detection task receives partial match events from its child tasks, it will have to determine whether a candidate event stored in the history table satisfies the condition together with the newly received information, which means that it will have to scan the records in the history table. Maintaining one history table for each system view instance will inevitably increase the size of the history table and thus increase the scanning time. A trade-off between time and space may be desirable, but is out of the scope of this dissertation.

5. Generating Workflow Tree

As we discussed earlier in this chapter, different workflow trees for a given signature may result in different performance. Three major factors that reflect the performance are the CPU time, the message transmission and the storage requirement. The less requirement for the three factors, the better performance the workflow tree can result in.

Theoretically, we can define the optimal workflow tree for a specific signature as the one with the least CPU usage, message transmission and space requirement, and use the optimal workflow tree to gain the best performance. However, this requires a measurement of the CPU usage, the message transmission and the space requirement by the specific signatures, which involves not only how message are transmitted but also how often each type of events in the specific signature occurs and how conditions are evaluated.

An interesting approach to achieve this is to develop a cost model that can estimate the aforementioned measurements and select the optimal workflow tree according to the model. However, the development of the cost model will inevitably involve calculating (or estimating) the frequency of various types of events, which is usually time-consuming, and the resulting model will depend on the systems that are used to generate the cost model and may change as time goes on.

In the following, we present an alternative approach that considers several heuristics that usually lead to "good" workflow trees.

5.1   A Heuristic Approach

In this subsection, we discuss three principles for developing effective workflow trees as well as their relationships, and then present the heuristic algorithm that generates workflow trees on the basis of the principles.

The edges in a workflow tree represent the required information flows in the detection process. An edge implies message transmission between two systems if the detection tasks for the two nodes involved in the edge are located at different systems. If one node requires another node, a path between them is certainly unavoidable. However, unnecessary edges may result in unnecessary message transmissions and additional storage.

Consider a specific signature with three nodes n_1, n_2, and n_3, where n_3 requires both node n_1 and n_2, and the system views associated with the three nodes belong to three different systems. This signature has two workflow trees shown in figures 7.2(b) and 7.2(c). The workflow tree in figure 7.2(b) is bad, since the variable values assigned at n_1 must be sent to n_3 through n_2, resulting in two message transmissions and additional storage at n_2. On the other hand, the workflow tree in figure 7.2(c) is better than the previous one, since it allows the variable values assigned at n_1 and n_2 to be sent to n_3 separately. This example suggests that a workflow tree should avoid unnecessary edges. Principle 7.1 states this observation.

PRINCIPLE 7.1 *Place an edge from node n_1 to node n_2 only when (1) n_1 requires n_2, or (2) n_1 requires node n' and there is a path from n_2 to n'.*

If the inclusion of the edges is unavoidable, the system views associated with the two nodes involved in an edge should at least be located at the component system so that the necessary information flow will be processed in the same local system instead of being transmitted between different systems. Principle 7.2 states this observation.

PRINCIPLE 7.2 *If there has to be a path between two nodes that belong to the same system, place an edge directly between them whenever possible.*

Different events usually occur at different rates. We call the events that happen infrequently the *rare events*. For example, the event represented by node n_1 in figure 6.1, which is a DOS attack, is a rare event, since such an event seldom happens in a normal network. Note that rare events are relative and context dependent. A type of events that is rare in one situation may not be rare in another.

Rare events can help improve workflow tree generation. Note that a partial match event is generated at node n only if n has received partial match events from n's child nodes. Since rare events occur infrequently, the nodes that have rare events as descendants tend to generate fewer partial match events than the other nodes. Indeed, the lower the the placement of the rare events in the workflow tree, the fewer partial match events will occur, and the less message transmission and storage are required. This leads to principle 7.3.

PRINCIPLE 7.3 *Place the nodes for rare events as close to the leaves as possible.*

There may be conflicts between the principles. For example, the workflow tree shown in figure 7.2(c) is better than the one in figure 7.2(b) according to principle 7.1. However, if event n_1 is extremely rare, it *may* be better to choose the latter one according to principle 7.3. To precisely decide which one

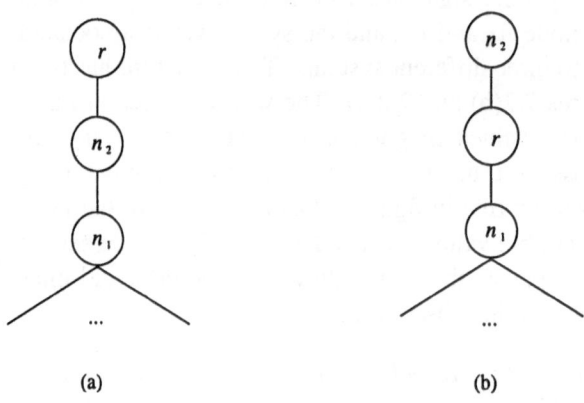

Figure 7.5. Comparason of two workflow trees

is better requires the cost of both workflow trees, which is what we wanted to avoid as discussed earlier.

Here we compare the three principles in normal situations and order them in terms of their priorities. First, let us compare principles 7.1 and 7.3 using the aforementioned example. Suppose n_1 is rare. At first glance, it seems that the workflow tree in figure 7.2(b) is much better than the one in figure 7.2(c). One reason could be that with the workflow tree in figure 7.2(b), detection task n_2 does not need to send messages to n_3 if it has not received anything from n_1. Moreover, if the history table of n_2 is limited to a certain size, some information may be dropped without being transmitted at all. However, this reasoning is flawed if we look at another aspect of this workflow tree. Note that n_2 does not require n_1, which implies that the information sent by detection task n_1 will not reduce the information stored in the history table of n_2. As a result, if we use the workflow tree in figure 7.2(b), each event detected by detection task n_1 will generate a partial match along with each tuple stored in the history table of n_2. The information sent to detection task n_3 is then the Cartesian product of the history tables of n_1 and n_2. In contrast, if the workflow tree in figure 7.2(c) is used, only the history tables need to be sent. Therefore, we assign principle 7.1 higher priority than principle 7.3. (Note that in extreme cases, i.e., when n_1 is *extremely* rare, the workflow tree in figure 7.2(b) may have less cost.) A similar reasoning can show that we should give higher priority to principle 7.1 than principle 7.2.

Now let us compare principles 7.2 and 7.3. Suppose r, n_1 and n_2 are three events (among others) involved in a signature. Assume that event r is rare, and events n_2 and n_3 are in the same component system. Figure 7.5(a) shows the workflow tree that we will select if principle 7.2 is given higher priority, and figure 7.5(b) shows the workflow tree that we will choose if we favor principle 7.3 over principle 7.2. With the workflow tree in figure 7.5(b), both n_1 and r need to transmit messages through the network in order to send information to their parent detection tasks. However, since event r is rare and it requires variables from its descendants, r will have much less partial matches than n_1, and the messages from r to n_2 will be much less than those from n_1 to r. In contrast, with the workflow tree in figure 7.5(a), only the messages from n_2 to r needs to be sent in the network, since n_1 and n_2 are located in the same component system. If we assume that sending messages from n_1 to r in the first case has roughly the same cost as transmitting messages from n_2 to r in the second case, then the workflow tree in figure 7.5(b) has a little more cost than the one in figure 7.5(a) in terms of message transmission. However, when detecting an attack, the workflow tree in figure 7.5(b) involves two messages between the component systems in which the three nodes are located, while the workflow tree in figure 7.5(a) only has one. Thus, the workflow tree in figure 7.5(b) introduces longer delay than the one in figure 7.5(a). Nevertheless, the workflow tree in figure 7.5(b) requires less space than the one in figure 7.5(a), since the partial match table of r in figure 7.5(b) will be smaller than that of n_2 in figure 7.5(a) due to the rareness of r. Here we care more about the speed of detection than the space requirement; thus, we decide to give principle 7.2 a higher priority. Principle 7.3 may have higher priority than principle 7.2 if space becomes a compelling concern.

Figure 7.6 shows the algorithm *Gen_WFT* developed according to these principles. The input of the algorithm consists of a specific signature S and a set *Rare* of the nodes corresponding to rare events, which is a subset of the nodes in S. The output of the algorithm is a workflow tree for S. The algorithm uses a subroutine *Gen_Tree* to help construct the target workflow tree. The algorithm *Gen_WFT* first generates the part of the workflow tree for the positive nodes and then the whole tree, ensuring that the processing of a positive event does not require the processing of any negative one(s).

In the subroutine *Gen_Tree*, the algorithm first constructs a set of trees according to the relationship *require*, the location where the events are observed, and the rare event information (steps 2 - 10). The algorithm always chooses a node that does not require any node not in R as the next candidate to be processed. Since the relation *require* is a strict partial order, the algorithm can always find a candidate event.

As shown in steps 4 - 7, the algorithm tries to find the nodes that will arrange the most number of nodes in one component system (principle 7.2), and then tries to find a rare event from them (principle 7.3). In steps 9 and 10, the algorithm adds edges only when necessary (principle 7.1).

After processing all of the input nodes, the subroutine *Gen_Tree* builds one single tree if the previous steps result in more than one tree (steps 11 - 15). The

---

Algorithm *Gen_WFT*
Input: A specific signature S and a subset $Rare$ of the nodes in S,
Output: A workflow tree T for S.
Method:
    1. Let $result :=$ an empty tree, $N =$ the set of positive nodes in S;
    2. Let $result := Gen\_Tree(S, result, N, Rare)$;
    3. Let $N :=$ the set of negative nodes in S;
    4. Let $result := Gen\_Tree(S, result, N, Rare)$;
    5. **return** $result$.

Subroutine *Gen_Tree*
Input: A specific signature S, a tree T_{in}, a subset N and a subset $Rare$ of
       the nodes in S.
Output: A tree T_{out}.
Method:
    1. Let $R := \{T_{in}\}$;
    2. **while** $N \neq \emptyset$ **do**
    3.   Let C be the set of nodes in N that do not require any node in N;
    4.   **for** each node n' in C, let its weight be the number of the trees in R
        that have nodes required by n' and whose roots are in the same
        component system as n';
    5.   let C' be the set of nodes in C that have the largest weight;
    6.   **if** $C' \cap Rare \neq \emptyset$, let $C' := C' \cap Rare$;
    7.   let n be any node in C';
    8.   Let $N := N - \{n\}$, $R := R \cup \{n\}$;
    9.   **for** each tree T in R that has nodes required by n **do**
    10.   Add an edge from n to T's root;
    11. **if** $|R| > 1$ (i.e. R has more than one tree)
    12.   Group the trees in R in such a way that the trees whose roots
        belong to the same component system are in one group;
    13.   Choose a group G that has the maximum number of trees;
    14.   **if** there is a tree T in G that has no common nodes with $Rare$,
            let $r := T$,
        else let r be any tree in G;
    15.   **for** each tree $T \neq r$ in R, add an edge from r's root to T's root; let
        result be the newly constructed tree;
    16. **return** $result$.

Figure 7.6. Generation of a workflow tree from a specific signature

algorithm chooses one of them and adds edges from its root to the roots of all the others. To minimize the message transmission, the algorithm chooses the tree whose root belongs to the component system having the most roots of the aforementioned trees (principle 7.2). Again, the algorithm places rare events as close to the leaves as possible by trying not to choose a tree that has nodes representing rare events (principle 7.3).

Chapter 8

CARDS: AN EXPERIMENTAL SYSTEM FOR DETECTING DISTRIBUTED ATTACKS

We have developed a proof-of-concept system named Coordinated Attack Response and Detection Systems (CARDS) to explore the feasibility of the approaches we have proposed. In this chapter, we report the design and the implementation issues as well as our experience of CARDS.

1. CARDS Architecture

CARDS is a distributed intrusion detection system composed of three kinds of independent but cooperative components: *signature manager*, *monitor* and *directory service*. Figure 8.1 shows the architecture of CARDS. In a typical environment, there may be one or more signature managers and monitors. The monitors can be embedded in the monitored system or as a dedicated monitor running on a separate system from the monitored system. Several monitors can cooperate with each other through message passing when they are involved in detecting one specific signature. A typical configuration of CARDS is depicted in Figure 8.2. The details of these components are presented in the following subsections.

1.1 Signature Manager

CARDS, Signature managers are the administrative components in CARDS. As shown in figure 8.1, with the monitor configuration information retrieved from the directory service, a signature manager (1) generates specific signatures from generic signatures, (2) decomposes specific signatures into intrusion detection tasks, and (3) distributes these tasks to the involved monitors.

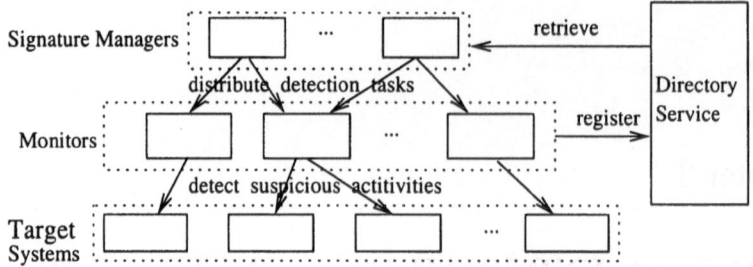

Figure 8.1. The CARDS architecture

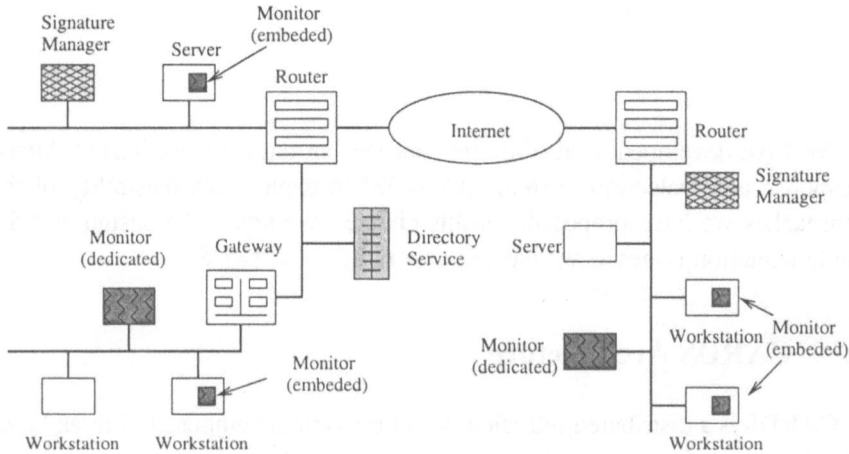

Figure 8.2. A typical configuration

The technical challenges involved in signature managers is how to generate specific signatures from generic one and how to decompose specific signatures into detection tasks. We have formally discussed detection task generation in Chapter 7. We will further discuss some implementation details in section 8.2.

The distribution of detection tasks can be carried out on the basis of existing transport services such as TCP. (The current implementation of CARDS is based TCP protocol using Socket.) In a real deployment, the communication between signature managers and monitors should be secured. In particular, the source and the content of each detection task should be authenticated. Encryption of detection tasks is not essential; however, in some extremely secure applications where it is not desirable for the enemy to know what the IDSs are doing, it might be necessary encrypt the detection tasks as well.

1.2   Monitor

The monitors are the components that carry out the intrusion detection tasks. In practice, each monitor is an application that can run on the monitored system or a separate system apart from the monitored system. Each monitor does audit information collection, filtering, reformatting as well as detecting the attacks. A monitor receives the detection task from a signature manager. During the process of executing a detecting attack, it may cooperate with other monitors as specified by the detection task.

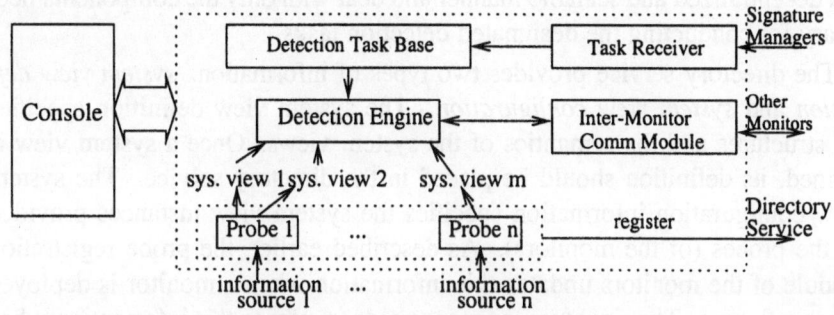

Figure 8.3.   The monitor architecture

Figure 8.3 shows the inner structure of a monitor, which is composed of one or more *probes*, a *detection engine*, an *inter-monitor communication module*, a *detection task base*, a *task receiver*, and a *console*.

Probes are responsible for collecting information from the target system, filtering and reformatting the information according to the system view as well as providing the results to the detection engine. Each probe gets information from one particular information source such as a host audit trail and the traffic on a network segment. While one monitor may have one or more probes, each probe may also provide one or more system views, each of which corresponds to one particular aspect of the information source. For example, a probe that gets information from the host audit trail may have two system views: one for the user's shell commands, and the other for the TCP connections that involve the host. The system view configuration of each probe (i.e., what system views each probe provides) should be registered in the directory service, which is later retrieved by signature managers to generate specific signatures.

The task receiver receives commands for adding or removing detection tasks from the signature manager, and then add or remove detection tasks from or to the detection task base accordingly.

The detection engine is the core module of the monitor that *executes* the detection tasks. When a detection task is derived from a specific signature involving several monitors, the detection engine cooperates with the detection engines in the related monitors by passing messages through the inter-monitor communication module. The console is the user interface of the monitor.

1.3 Directory Service

The directory service is the central place for providing system-wide information to both signature managers and monitors. Although the directory service may be distributed or replicated, they function as a single component of CARDS. Thus, the signature managers and the monitors are allowed to work in a decentralized and scalable manner and deal with only the components necessary for conducting the designated detection tasks.

The directory service provides two types of information: *system view definition* and *system view configuration*. The system view definition specifies the structures and the semantics of the system views. Once a system view is defined, its definition should be placed in the directory service. The system view configuration information specifies the system view instances provided by the probes (of the monitors). As described earlier, the probe registration module of the monitors updates this information when a monitor is deployed or reconfigured. The signature manager needs to refer to this information when it generates specific signatures.

The purpose of the directory service is to make our system scalable. Since distributed attacks usually consist of several sessions that spread across several systems and cannot be reliably detected from a single place, the monitors that detect them should be installed at various places, possibly across several different administrative domains. To achieve the scalability, interoperability, and distribution of the system, we adopt the directory service to provide global information that needs to be shared by the signature managers and the monitors. As a result, the signature managers and the monitors are allowed to work in a decentralized way and deal with only the components that are necessary to perform the designated detection tasks.

The directory service is critical for the scalability of the IDS. It allows the signature managers and the monitors to work in a decentralized and scalable manner and deal with only the components necessary for conducting the designated detection tasks. However, the unavailability of the directory service does not affect the cooperation of monitors; instead, it only prevents signature managers from generating specific signatures. Nevertheless, if possible, the directory service should be replicated and distributed (using, for example, LDAP replication server) to provide better availability.

2. System Design Issues

In this section, we discuss the approaches that signature managers use to generate and decompose specific signatures and the procedures with which monitors cooperatively detect the coordinated attacks. Theoretical aspect of this work has been discussed in [Ning et al., 2001]. Here we focus on system aspects and discuss the design and implementation issues in the framework of CARDS.

2.1　Internal Languages

Since CARDS is a distributed IDS consisting of multiple components that need to communicate with each other, it is necessary to enable different components to understand each other. In other words, CARDS components need some common languages. Due to the rich semantics typically involved in the cooperation of signature managers and monitors, simple agreements are usually not good enough to provide the necessary support. In addition, for the convenience of configuration and ease of experiments, it is desirable that the messages between CARDS components are not only computer comprehensible, but also human readable.

As discussed in chapter 2, several efforts are under way to establish some common languages (e.g., IDMEF [Curry and Debar, 2001]) for IDSs. However, all the existing results do not cover the ground required by CARDS components. This is because all the existing results do not consider any specific mechanisms to decompose, distribute, and coordinate decentralized intrusion detection activities, which are central issues studied in CARDS. Thus, we decided to develop a set of internal languages for the CARDS components.

Our internal languages are based on eXtensible Markup Language (XML) [Bray et al., 1998]. We chose XML as the foundation of the internal languages due to the following reasons: (1) XML is not only computer comprehensible, but also human readable; (2) XML is widely accepted in many areas (e.g., IDMEF [Curry and Debar, 2001]) and could help in possible future technology transfer; (3) There are rich API supports for XML related development (e.g., Apache's Xerces parsers).

We defined Document Type Definitions (DTDs) for system views, signatures, and detection tasks. Due to space reasons, we cannot include the details of these DTDs in this paper. Figures 8.4 through 8.6 show example XML representations (with some details omitted) of system views, signatures and detection tasks, respectively.

The current focus of CARDS is to examine the decentralized detection procedure proposed in [Ning et al., 2001]; thus, view definition is not supported yet. We plan to develop the corresponding DTD for view definition when we need to perform the related experiments. In addition, the DTD for signatures does not support complex qualitative temporal relationships between events (e.g., e_1 (before OR during) e_2); however, this feature does not affect the decentralized detection very much and can be easily incorporated into the current DTD.

```
<?xml version="1.0" standalone="no" ?>
<!DOCTYPE system_view SYSTEM "http://infosec/sysview.dtd">
<system_view name="TCPDOSAttacks">
    <event_schema>
        <attribute name="VictimIP" type="varchar" len="15"/>
        <attribute name="VictimPort" type="int" len="1"/>
    </event_schema>
</system_view>
```

Figure 8.4.   The system view *TCPDOSAttacks*

2.2   Specific Signature Generation

One of the central tasks of signature managers is to generate specific signatures from a generic one. For the sake of presentation, we first define some terms. We say that a probe *has* the system view *v* if the probe provides information through *v*. We say a system view instance *v* of a signature is *associated* with the probe *p* of the monitor *m* if *p* is designated to provide information for the signature through *v*. In CARDS, a signature is called a specific signature if each system view instance of the signature is associated with a probe of a monitor in the system. Thus, the task of generating specific signatures from a generic one is to associate all the system view instances of the signature with the probes of the monitors in the system.

When generating specific signatures from a generic one, the signature manager first looks up in the directory service for the probes that have the system views whose instances are used in the generic signature. Then the signature manager derives specific signatures by associating the system view instances with the probes of the monitors under its control. For example, consider the signature shown in figure 6.1. Suppose there are a signature manager and three monitors called *Sniffer*, *Megalon* and *Backeast*. If the signature manager learns by looking up the directory service that the three monitors have three probes *DOSProbe*, *MegalonTCPProbe*, and *BackeastTCPProbe* that have the system view *TCPDOSAttacks*, *LocalTCPConn*, and *LocalTCPConn*, respectively, then it can generate a specific signature by associating the *SysView1*, *SysView2*, and *SysView3* with these probes. This specific signature then describes the Mitnick attack against the hosts monitored by *Megalon* and *Backeast*.

One generic signature usually generates more than one specific signature, since the attacks modeled by the generic signature may happen against different targets. In the previous example, we can generate another specific signature by associating *SysView2* with *BackeastTCPProbe* and *SysView3* with *MegalonTCPProbe*, which represents a different attacking strategy against the two hosts. In addition, there may be other hosts being monitored, and the Mitnick

```
<?xml version="1.0" standalone="no"?>
<!DOCTYPE signature SYSTEM "http://infosec/signature.dtd">
<signature name="mitnick">
    <node name="n1">
        <system_view_inst name="SysView1"/>
        <assignment>
            <variable name = "var_IP"/> <attribute name="VictimIP"/>
        </assignment>
        ...
    </node>
    <node name="n2">
        <system_view_inst name="SysView2"/>
        <assignment>
            <variable name="var_SrcIP"/> <attribute name="SrcIP"/>
        </assignment>
        ...
        <timed_condition>
            <and>
                <equal>
                    <attribute name="SrcIP"/> <var_ref name="var_IP"/>
                </equal>
                ...
            </and>
        </timed_condition>
    </node>
    <node name="n3" type="negative">
        <system_view_inst name="SysView3"/>
        <timed_condition> ... </timed_condition>
    </node>
    <edge from="n2" to="n1" label="younger"/>
    <edge from="n3" to="n2" label="equal"/>
    <declare_sys_view_inst name="SysView1"
                           system_view="DOSAttacks"/>
    <declare_sys_view_inst name="SysView2" ... />
    <declare_sys_view_inst name="SysView3" ... />
</signature>
```

Figure 8.5. The generic signature for the Mitnick attack (some details omitted)

attack may be launched against these hosts as well. Thus, the signature manager should associate the system view instances of a generic signature with all combinations of probes where the attack may happen to the targets monitored by the probes.

Consider the generic signature for the Mitnick attack shown in figure 6.1. Suppose in the directory service the monitors and the probes that support the system views underlying the signature are as shown in Table 8.1. When gen-

```
<?xml version="1.0" standalone="no" ?>
<!DOCTYPE task SYSTEM "http://infosec/task.dtd">
<task name="n2" root="yes" spec_sig_name="mitnick_1" type="positive">
    <system_view_inst name="SysView2" system_view="LocalTCPConn">
        <monitor baseport="4200" location="129.174.142.177" name="m2"/>
        <probe name="LocalTCPConn"/>
    </system_view_inst>
    <partial_match_table>
        <PMT_attribute len="1" name="var_DstPort" source="assign"
                source_attr="DstPort" type="int"/>
        ...
    </partial_match_table>
    <timed_condition> ... </timed_condition>
    <parent_node name="n3">
        <monitor baseport="4200" location="129.174.142.140" name="m3"/>
    </parent_node>
    <child_node name="n1">
        <monitor baseport="4200" location="129.174.142.140" name="m1"/>
        <child_partial_match_table>
            <child_PMT_attribute name="begin_time_n1" ... />
            <child_PMT_attribute name="end_time_n1" ... />
            <child_PMT_attribute name="var_IP" ... />
            <child_PMT_attribute name="var_Port" ... />
        </child_partial_match_table>
    </child_node>
    <negative_root_node name="n3">
        <monitor baseport="4200" location="129.174.142.140" name="m3"/>
        <negative_root_partial_match_table>
            <negative_root_PMT_attribute name="end_time_n3" .../>
            ...
        </negative_root_partial_match_table>
    </negative_root_node>
</task>
```

Figure 8.6. Detection task n_2 of a specific signature for the Mitnick attack (some details omitted)

erating specific signatures for the Mitnick attack, the signature manager first retrieves this information from the directory service and then associate the system view instances of the generic signature with the probes in all possible combinations that the Mitnick attack may happen. For this particular probe configuration, the signature manager will generate 12 specific signatures, with *SysView1* associated with the probe *DOSProbe* at the monitor *Sniffer*, and *SysView2* and *SysView3* with all combinations of the rest of the probes.

Some optimization may be achieved using the timed condition. In the above example, the specific signature that associates *SysView2* with *MegalonTCP-*

Table 8.1.   A list of monitors, probes and their system views

Monitor	Probe	System View
Sniffer	DOSProbe	TCPDOSAttacks
Megalon	MegalonTCPProbe	LocalTCPConn
Meadow	MeadowTCPProbe	LocalTCPConn
Infosec	InfosecTCPProbe	LocalTCPConn
Backeast	BackeastTCPProbe	LocalTCPConn

Probe and *SysView3* with *BackeastTCPProbe* needs to be generated only if the host monitored by *Megalon* trusts the host monitored by *Backeast*. Unfortunately, such optimization can only be performed manually in the current version of CARDS.

The reader may have noticed a potential problem with the specific signature generation: There could be too many specific signatures due to the combinatorial nature of the generation procedure. Although we have argued that an attack can potentially happen to each of the specific signatures, having too many specific signatures may introduce severe performance penalty into the system. One method to alleviate the problem is to introduce the notion of *managed domain*, which restricts the number of monitored nodes in each domain. Moreover, it is worth noting that in reality, people care more about protecting critical resources such as gateways and file servers. Thus, it is desirable to have certain ways (e.g., a policy language) with which the system administrator can describe what (combinations of) systems should be protected. Such methods can help reduce the number of specific signatures; however, they are out of the scope of this paper.

2.3   Specific Signature Decomposition

In [Ning et al., 2001] we have discussed various choices of specific signature decomposition as well as the related issues, and developed an approach to decomposing specific signatures into detection tasks. This approach has been used in the implementation of CARDS. In the following, we first briefly describe this approach and then give some details about its implementation in CARDS.

A serializable signature can be decomposed with a given workflow tree. The idea of signature decomposition is to have each node (i.e., event) of the signature as a basic execution unit, that is, a detection task, and coordinate these detection tasks to detect the distributed attacks represented by the signature.

The first step of signature decomposition is to transform the qualitative temporal relationships represented by the labeled arcs into specific conditions and incorporate them into the timed conditions. This is done using timestamp variables. For each node n, we add two additional assignments: $begin\_time\_n :=$ $begin\_time$ and $end\_time\_n := end\_time$, where $begin\_time$ and end_time are the interval-based timestamp. (Since timestamps contain critical time information of the events, we perform the assignments even if no labeled arc involves the node (event).) If there is a labeled arc from n_1 to n_2, for example, n_1 before n_2, the labeled arc can be transformed into $end\_time\_n_1 <$ $begin\_time\_n_2$. We say a node n is the least common ancestor of n_1 and n_2 if n is ancestor of both n_1 and n_2 and no descendant of n is their common ancestor. Then we modify the timed condition associated with the least common ancestor of n_1 and n_2 as the conjunction of the previous timed condition and $end\_time\_n_1 < begin\_time\_n_2$.

Since all the nodes in a signature are related to each other via variable assignments, a critical job in decomposing a signature is to identify what information of a detection task is required by other detection tasks through variables. This can be done by a depth-first traversal of the given workflow tree. To do this, we associate with each node n two sets: $RequiredSet_n$ which contains variables required by n's ancestors, and $ProvidedSet_n$ which contains variables assigned at n and n's descendants. It is easy to see that the variables that a node n needs to send to its parent is $ProvidedSet_n \cap RequiredSet_n$.

To assist in the computation of $ProvidedSet_n$ and $RequiredSet_n$ for each node n, we associate with n two additional sets: $AssignedSet_n$ which contains the set of variables assigned at n, and $NeededSet_n$ which contains the set of variables used in the timed condition of n. Both $AssignedSet_n$ and $NeededSet_n$ can be easily computed for each node n.

Initially, $RequiredSet_{root} = \emptyset$ and $ProvidedSet_l = AssignedSet_l$, where l is a leaf node. When traversing down the workflow tree, each node n passes $RequiredSet_n$ to its chid nodes along with the variables directly used in its timed condition. In other words, n's child node n' will have $RequiredSet_{n'} =$ $RequiredSet_n \cup NeededSet_n$. When traversing up the workflow tree, each node n gets $ProvidedSet_{n'}$ for all child nodes n', and thus $ProvidedSet_n =$ $\cup_{\forall n's\,child\,n'} ProvidedSet_{n'} \cup AssignedSet_n$. It then returns $ProvidedSet_n$ to its parent.

Once the variables that each node needs to send to its parent node are identified, the corresponding signature can be easily decomposed. In order to cooperate with other detection tasks, each detection task should also remember where it should get events from (i.e., the probe associated with the corresponding system view instance), the condition that it should check against each observed event (i.e., the transformed timed condition), what variables it will receive from each child detection task, and what variables it should send to its parent detection task. Figure 8.6 shows a detection task decomposed from a specific version of the signature in figure 8.5. (Due to space reasons, we cannot show all the detection tasks decomposed from the signature.)

3. Prototype Implementation

We have implemented a prototype of CARDS according to the design discussed earlier. The goal of this version is to examine the feasibility of our approach and understand the issues possibly involved. To focus on the new mechanisms proposed in our work, we made several simplifications to reduce the development time and cost. In particular, we assume that the components of CARDS can successfully establish trust and communicate securely with each other.

The current version of CARDS is mostly written in Java, with a few probes written in C++ and incorporated into the system via Java Native Interface (JNI). Xerces Java Parser 1.0.0 is used to process the XML documents representing system views, signatures as well as detection tasks. Since secure communication between the components is not the focus of this system, message transmission between components is carried out over TCP.

In the following, we discuss the implementation issues related to the current prototype.

3.1 Directory Service and *DirHelper*

Directory service is a critical component for CARDS to achieve scalability. It stores two kinds of information: system view definitions and system view configurations. There are multiple options in implementing the directory service in CARDS: We can use an existing directory service (e.g., Open LDAP directory server, Microsoft Active Directory Service) through standard directory access protocols (e.g., X.500 and LDAP (Lightweight Directory Access Protocol)), or implement a specific directory service for CARDS, or even use a replicated database management system. To make CARDS independent of any specific directory service product, we separate the directory service from the rest of CARDS by introducing a helper component *DirHelper*. That is, each signature manager (or monitor) has a *DirHelper* as a local component, and whenever it needs to access the directory service, it does so by invoking the corresponding methods of *DirHelper*.

Each *DirHelper* provides methods for signature managers or monitors to interact with the directory service, including initializing the directory service, registering/retrieving/removing system views/probes, listing monitors/probes by system views, and listing all monitors/probes in the directory service.

The current version of *DirHelper* stores the information in a Microsoft SQL Server 7.0 database, which is used as a directory server. Thus, the current version of directory service is certainly not replicated nor scalable. This is to reduce the development time and cost. As shown by our experiments, such a directory service has little impact on the performance for small-scale deployment of CARDS. We plan to replace the database service with replicated directory service (e.g., replicated Open LDAP directory server) that supports LDAP when it is time to examine CARDS in large-scale systems. The replacement of directory server is expected not to affect the rest of the system.

3.2   Signature Manager

A signature manager is further divided into the Graphical User Interface (GUI), the specific signature generator, the (detection) task generator, and the (detection) task distributor. The signature manager accesses the directory through *DirHelper*. The mechanisms of specific signature generator and task generator, i.e., how to generate specific signatures and detection tasks, have been discussed in sections 8.2.2 and 8.2.3, respectively. Figure 8.7 shows a screen shot of the signature manager.

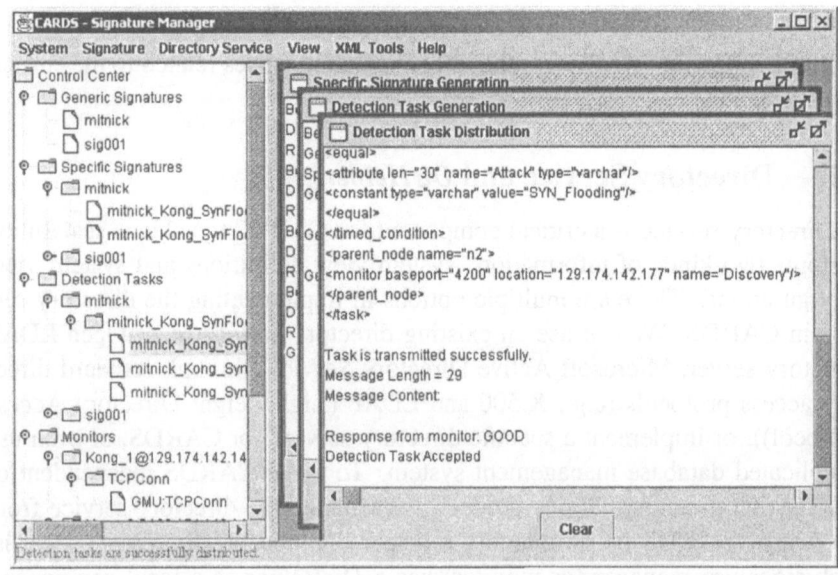

Figure 8.7.   The screen shot of a signature manager

When generating a specific signature, the specific signature generator retrieves the "contact" information of each monitor involved in the signature. This "contact" information consists of the IP address and a TCP port number, which is called *TaskReceiverPort*. Once started, each monitor will dedicate a thread, which is called *TaskReceiver*, to listen at the *TaskReceiverPort* for possible incoming task distribution. The same information will be passed to detection tasks when the specific signature is decomposed.

Task distributor distributes the generated detection tasks to the monitors indicated in the tasks, removes obsolete tasks from monitors, or queries the tasks installed in monitors. The protocol between a signature manager and a monitor, which is carried out by the task distributor on the signature manager side and the task receiver on the monitor side, is a one-round request-reply protocol. That is, the signature manager sends a request message to the monitor and receives a response message from the monitor. Each message starts with a length field which indicates the length of the message in bytes (excluding the length field). The rest of the message is a character string as explained as follows.

The message from a signature manager to a monitor consists of three parts: (1) the name of the signature manager, (2) the command, which is one of "ADD", "DELETE", and "QUERY", and (3) the data to be transmitted. The three parts are separated by a special separating character. When the command is "ADD", the data is an XML document representing the detection task. When the command is "DELETE", the data further consists of two parts separated by the special separating character, i.e. a specific signature name followed by a task name. When the command is "QUERY", the data section is empty.

For the "ADD" and "DELETE" commands, the reply from the monitor to the signature manager consists of two sections separated by the special separating character: (1) status and (2) message. Status is either "GOOD" or "BAD", while message is a human readable message (error message when status = "BAD").

For the "QUERY" command, the structure of the reply message consists of the length followed by a list of pairs, each of which consists of a specific signature name and a task name. Again, these logical entities are separated by the special separating character.

3.3 Monitor

Due to its need to process multiple tasks (e.g., monitoring local events, communicating with other monitors and signature managers), monitor is implemented as a multi-threaded application. Each monitor consists of the following threads: the main thread that controls all the other threads, the *TaskReceiver* thread that receives the detection tasks distributed by signature managers, the communication thread that communicates with other monitors, one thread for each active detection task, and one thread for each local probe. The GUI (i.e., the console in figure 8.3) and the detection task base are implemented as common modules that can interact with all the threads if necessary. The component

Detection Engine shown in figure 8.3 is virtually implemented as the collection of the active detection tasks. Figure 8.8 shows a screen shot of a monitor.

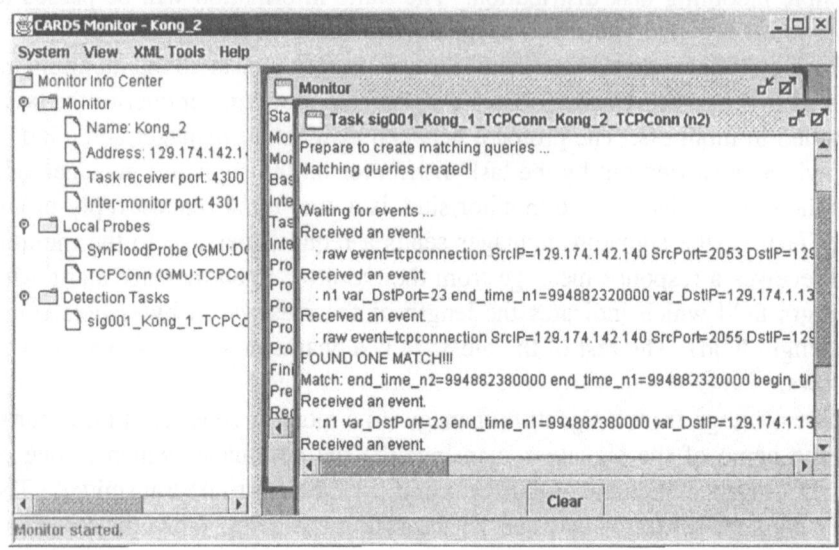

Figure 8.8. The screen shot of a monitor

Detection Engine and Detection Tasks

As discussed earlier, detection engine is virtually implemented as the collection of all active detection tasks. A detection task stored in the detection task base is activated when the monitor starts; a detection task distributed to an active monitor is started immediately after it is validated.

Each detection task is indeed an event handler. It processes the raw events generated by local probes or partial match events sent by other detection tasks, which may be located in the same monitor or a remote monitor. The detection task that processes raw events needs to be registered to the corresponding local probes so that the probe will directly dispatch the raw events to it. Similarly, the inter-monitor communication module has access to the list of active detection tasks so that it can dispatch the partial match events, which may be from local detection tasks or remote ones, to the right detection tasks.

Each event is represented as an event message, which is a string consisting of an event type followed by a sequence of name-value pairs. The event type and the name-value pairs are separated with a space. The event type is either "raw", which says the corresponding event is a raw event generated by a probe, or the name of the child detection task, which means that the corresponding event is a partial match event sent by the child detection task. The name-value pairs describe the attributes of the event. For example, the following is an event message, which gives the attribute values describing a TCP connection.

```
raw event=tcpconnection SrcIP=129.174.142.140
SrcPort=2053 DstIP=129.174.1.13 DstPort=23
begin_time=994882358933 end_time=994882362856
```

Note that the event message format is selected to simplify the prototype implementation. In a deployable implementation, we may have to choose more efficient and interoperable encoding method (e.g., octet string).

To reduce the development cost of this prototype system, we transform the event processing procedures in each detection task into SQL queries and use DBMS (which is Microsoft SQL Server 7.0) to execute them. Our experiments showed that such a choice did have noticeable impact to the performance; however, the performance penalty is acceptable for testing the coordination of multiple CARDS components. Note that the choice of DBMS in the prototype implementation does not imply that our approach has to rely on DBMS or SQL engine to perform the event handling. We plan to replace the DBMS-based event handler with a more efficient one when it is time to improve the performance of each detection task.

Inter-Monitor Communication Module

The monitor relies on the inter-monitor communication module (or simply communication module) to interact with other monitors. More precisely, the local detection tasks of each monitor communicate with the relevant remote detection tasks through the communication module. When a monitor is running, the communication module, which executes as a thread, listens at the inter-monitor communication port called *CommPort* for incoming messages. In addition, the communication module can also be invoked by local detection tasks through method invocation when the local detection tasks need to send messages.

When a local detection task needs to send an event message to another detection task, it submits the message to the local communication module along with the IP address, the port number, the name of the corresponding specific signature and the name of the target detection task through method invocation. If the event message is destined to another local detection task, the communication module will simply pass it to the target detection task by invoking the event receiving method of the local detection task. Otherwise, the communication module will establish a TCP connection with the communication module of the target monitor and transmit the event message along with the names of the specific signature and the detection task.

When the communication module receives a message, it parses the message to find out the names of the specific signature and the detection task. Then it performs a table lookup to locate the corresponding detection task and passes the event message by invoking the event receiving method of the target detection task.

The protocol between monitors (or communication modules of monitors) is quite simple. It is a one-way protocol; each message is encoded as a string, which consists of the name of the specific signature, the name of the target detection task, the event message. The three logical components are separated by end-of-line (EOL) character.

Probes and Probe Loader

Probes observe security relevant data (e.g., audit trails, network traffic) and provide the data in unified forms through system views. They are critical components that make our approach independent of specific data collection mechanisms. The abstraction-based approach in [Ning et al., 2001] allows probes to either directly collect audit data from the data sources (e.g., network traffic, system call traces) or extract information from the detection of certain signatures via view definition. However, the latter feature is not implemented in the current prototype, but considered as a part of future implementation plan.

Probes are designed as configurable, plug-in modules. Monitor loads probes through a module named *ProbeLoader*. When a monitor is started, the *ProbeLoader* reads the configuration information of all the available probes, and then locates and loads the corresponding code into the monitor. For example, the following is the configuration information for the probe SynFloodProbe. It says the probe provides the system view SynFloodAttack, the code for the probe is edu.gmu.cards.probes.SynFloodProbe, which can be found in the Java Virtual Machine's class path, and there is no argument to be passed to the probe code.

```
Probe2.name=SynFloodProbe
Probe2.systemView=TCPDOSAttacks
Probe2.className=edu.gmu.cards.probes.SynFloodProbe
Probe2.numOfArgs=0
```

In the current prototype, each probe is dedicated to a specific information source, which collects the event and state information from that information source and reformats the information according to the specific system view(s). We developed several network based probes, including *TCPPacket* (the probe for TCP packets), *LocalTCPConn* (the probe for the TCP connections involving the local host), *TCPConnection* (the probe for all the observable TCP connections), and *SYNFloodProbe* (the probe for SYN flooding attacks). These probes are implemented by putting a wrapper around the well-known network traffic analysis tool, TCPDump [McCanne et al.,]. Thanks to the Windows version of TCP Dump (i.e., WinDump [Degioanni et al.,]), the probes we developed can run on both Unix platforms and Microsoft Windows.

There are other desirable information sources for which probes should be developed. Examples include host audit trails (e.g., Sun Solaris BSM audit trails [BSM,]), information collected by network management systems and provided through, for example, SNMP or RMON [Stallings, 1999], as well as alerts from other security relevant systems (e.g., firewalls and other IDSs). From the perspective of detecting attacks, it is desirable to have more information sources available, since different sources usually have complementary information. Nevertheless, one may not want to deploy all available probes in all the places because of the performance reasons.

3.4   Limitations

One important feature of CARDS is that the intrusion detection task is distributed over all the IDS components that observe the intrusion related data, and these components communicate with each other only when necessary. As a result, the communication cost required for intrusion detection is greatly reduced. We have conducted experiments for a limited number of distributed attacks in small-scale systems. The results showed the feasibility of signature decomposition and the distribution and execution of detection tasks. Further results in large distributed systems are needed to evaluate the scalability of the proposed approaches.

The experience with the current version of CARDS also shows several limitations of the approach. Some of the limitations are specific to the current implementation due to the prototype nature of the system and can be addressed easily in future implementation effort, while some others are more essential and require further research effort.

First, when generating specific signatures, CARDS tries to map a generic signature to all combinations of monitors that provide the system view instances underlying the generic signature. This will generate a large number of specific signatures even in a medium scale distributed system. As we discussed earlier, this approach does not consider the relationship between the underlying systems that the monitors are protecting, and not all of the specific signatures correspond to attacks that may cause severe damages. In reality, we may choose to detect some of the possible attacks and tolerate others due to some administrative concerns. Future work is needed to address this issue.

Second, the experience with CARDS revealed another issue about time other than the clock discrepancy problem. Even if the clocks of all the component systems in a distributed system are well synchronized, there are still problems involving time because of the network latency and multi-process nature of the contemporary operating systems. For example, the same TCP connection will not be labeled with the exact same timestamp on the two end-point computers that are far enough from each other. Even if the network latency is negligible, the timestamps may still be different if the workload of the two computers are very different. These observations imply that we have to properly deal with the timestamps of the events.

A simple countermeasure is to set up a threshold t as the maximum time difference and handle timestamps in a relaxed way. For example, two time points t_1 and t_2 in two different places are considered "equal" if $|t_1 - t_2| < t$, and t_1 is considered "before" t_2 if $t_1 - t < t_2$. A higher threshold will certainly help to tolerate worse clock discrepancy, but it will also result in a higher false alarm rate.

Third, the abstraction-based approach certainly introduces overhead in processing the events observed from target systems, though it can hide the difference between heterogeneous platforms. The overhead comes from the preprocessing of the events, which normally involves reformatting the events. Sometimes, there may not be direct correspondence between events observed on different platforms, and a probe may need to perform aggregation and other simple event processing before it can present an event on a system view. The hierarchical abstraction framework, which was proposed as a part of the abstraction-based approach in [Ning et al., 2001], gives a partial solution to this problem, though it is not implemented in the current version of CARDS.

Fourth, the communication between CARDS components is based on the TCP protocol. Though we did not experience any problem during the experiments, we realize the possibility that the CARDS components may not be able to communicate with each other as in the normal situation if the system is under attacks from some powerful enemies. This is actually a realistic problem for all the distributed IDSs. An ideal solution is to provide some special communication channels between IDS components; however, this is the same as requiring a separate network for IDS components, and this very separate network may be subject to attacks as well. Another approach is to let IDS components rely on simpler communication mechanisms such as UDP. However, the reliability of the message transmission must be taken care of as well.

A closely related issue is how to perform intrusion detection if some of the component IDSs or the communication channels are not reliable. The current version of CARDS may miss critical attacks or generate false alarms if the above situations happen. Indeed, this problem is not unique to CARDS, but common to all distributed systems. Additional research is required to address this problem.

Finally, with our current approach the IDS has to wait for the completion of the observed events before it can detect any attack. For example, if a signature involves a TCP connection, the corresponding event will not be generated until the connection is closed or broken. Indeed, this implies that an attack cannot be detected until after all the positive events involved in the attack complete.

A counter measure is to let the probe to report the starting and the ending points of an event separately. Although the IDS may not always be able to detect the attack if the ending times of certain positive events are critical to the existence of the attack, the IDS can often reason about the attack at an early stage. However, additional research is needed to implement this method efficiently.

Chapter 9

CONCLUSION

In this monograph we have presented an abstraction-based approach to intrusion detection in distributed systems, where the component systems are usually heterogeneous and/or autonomous. To address heterogeneity and autonomy of distributed environments, the concept of system view was introduced to provide an abstract interface between different heterogeneous and autonomous systems. This concept borrows the idea from multi-databases that different database management systems share the schema-level information (i.e., the structure of the data) among each other. However, due to the semantics of intrusion detection, the notion of system view in our setting differs from its counter part in multi-databases in that it should be able to include the schema-level information about the system state as well. In general, system views serve two purposes. First, system views hide the difference between heterogeneous systems. Second, they describe what information an autonomous system is willing to provide to other system. System views constitute the foundation of the approaches to distributed intrusion detection presented in this monograph.

In order to help different IDSs communicate effectively and efficiently, this monograph studied how to enable an IDS to request specific information from another IDS. It was proposed to represent a request for an IDS as a pattern among the events provided by the IDS plus a transformation rule, where the pattern specifies the events that the requesting party is interested in and the transformation rule extracts interesting information from the events. This result indeed gives IDSs the ability to ask queries from each other. This approach may not be helpful to represent the "regular" requests that one IDS may send to another one, since such requests can be predefined and standardized among all IDSs. However, it is useful to represent dynamic requests that cannot be predicted or too complex to predefine. We have shown an example in which the formal approach was used to add a query facility to the language (Common

Intrusion Specification Language (CISL)) of the Common Intrusion Detection Framework (CIDF).

To coordinate different IDSs to correlate distributed events, we have presented techniques to represent the event correlation to be performed as a pattern (i.e., signature) among distributed events. A novel, decentralized method was then presented for autonomous but cooperative IDSs to perform the event correlation specified by signatures. Specifically, a signature is decomposed into finer units called *detection tasks*, each of which represents the activity to be monitored in one place. The IDSs (involved in a signature) then perform the detection tasks cooperatively according to the "dependency" relationships among these tasks. Our approach is superior to the existing centralized or hierarchical approaches in that (1) communication is more efficient by having different IDSs communicate with each other only when necessary, and (2) no centralized or hierarchical trust is required (trust is also decentralized in our approach). As an important application of distributed event correlation, this approach can be used to represent and detect distributed (or coordinated) attacks that cannot be detected from a single place.

The experimental system CARDS provides a test-bed for the approach to distributed intrusion detection proposed in this work. In CARDS, specification of distributed attacks are separated from the detection of the attacks. Distributed attacks are described by generic signatures, which are common to all systems that provide the system views underlying the signatures. To protect specific systems, generic signatures are first mapped to specific signatures using the system configuration information, and then specific signatures are decomposed into detection tasks, which are distributed to and executed by the cooperative component IDSs. Our experience with CARDS showed the feasibility of the abstraction-based approach.

Appendix A
Document Type Definitions (DTDs) Used in CARDS

1.   The DTD for System Views

```
<!ENTITY % global_name "name NMTOKEN #REQUIRED">
<!ENTITY % local_name "name ID #REQUIRED">
<!ENTITY % attr_type "type (int | float | varchar)">
<!ENTITY % attr_len "len NMTOKEN #REQUIRED">

<!ELEMENT system_view (event_schema, predicate_set?, description?)>
<!ATTLIST system_view %global_name;>
<!ELEMENT event_schema (attribute+)>
<!ELEMENT attribute (possible_value*)>
<!ATTLIST attribute %local_name; %attr_type; "varchar" %attr_len;>
<!ELEMENT possible_value EMPTY>
<!ATTLIST possible_value value CDATA #REQUIRED>
<!ELEMENT predicate_set (predicate+)>
<!ELEMENT predicate (parameter*)>
<!ATTLIST predicate %local_name;>
<!ELEMENT parameter EMPTY>
<!ATTLIST parameter %local_name; %attr_type; "varchar" %attr_len;>
<!ELEMENT description (#PCDATA)>
<!ATTLIST description organization NMTOKEN "csis.gmu.edu"
                      developer CDATA #IMPLIED
                      contact CDATA #IMPLIED>
```

2.   The DTD for Signatures

```
<!ENTITY % global_name    "name  NMTOKEN #REQUIRED">
<!ENTITY % local_name_def "name  ID #REQUIRED">
<!ENTITY % local_name_ref "name IDREF #REQUIRED">
<!ENTITY % element_choice "(var_ref | attribute | constant)">
<!ENTITY % attr_type "type (int | float | varchar)">
<!ENTITY % attr_default_type "varchar">
```

```
<!ELEMENT signature (node, (node | edge)*, declare_sys_view_inst+)>
<!ATTLIST signature %global_name; generic_name NMTOKEN #IMPLIED>
<!ELEMENT node (system_view_inst, (assignment)*, timed_condition)>
<!ATTLIST node %local_name_def; type (positive | negative) "positive">
<!ATTLIST node rare (yes|no) "no">
<!ELEMENT system_view_inst EMPTY>
<!ATTLIST system_view_inst %local_name_ref;>
<!ELEMENT assignment (variable, attribute)>
<!ELEMENT variable EMPTY>
<!ATTLIST variable %local_name_def;>
<!ELEMENT attribute EMPTY>
<!ATTLIST attribute %global_name;>
<!ELEMENT constant EMPTY>
<!ATTLIST constant value CDATA #REQUIRED %attr_type; "varchar" >
<!ELEMENT var_ref EMPTY>
<!ATTLIST var_ref %local_name_ref;>
<!-- Begin timed condition -->
<!ENTITY % cond "(and | or | not | equal | greater_than | greater_equal
    | less_than | less_equal | not_equal | predicate)">
<!ELEMENT timed_condition %cond;>
<!ELEMENT and (%cond;, %cond;)>
<!ELEMENT or (%cond;, %cond;)>
<!ELEMENT not %cond;>
<!ELEMENT equal (%element_choice;, %element_choice;)>
<!ELEMENT greater_than (%element_choice;, %element_choice;)>
<!ELEMENT greater_equal (%element_choice;, %element_choice;)>
<!ELEMENT less_than (%element_choice;, %element_choice;)>
<!ELEMENT less_equal (%element_choice;, %element_choice;)>
<!ELEMENT not_equal (%element_choice;, %element_choice;)>
<!ELEMENT predicate (parameter*)>
<!ATTLIST predicate %global_name; time (begin|end|exist|forall)
   #REQUIRED>
<!ELEMENT parameter %element_choice;>
<!-- End timed condition -->
<!ELEMENT edge EMPTY>
<!ATTLIST edge from IDREF #REQUIRED to IDREF #REQUIRED
               label (equal | before | meets | overlaps |
                      during | starts | finishes) #REQUIRED>
<!-- Begin declare system view instances -->
<!ELEMENT declare_sys_view_inst (monitor, probe)?>
<!ATTLIST declare_sys_view_inst %local_name_def;
                                system_view NMTOKEN #REQUIRED>
<!ELEMENT monitor EMPTY>
<!ATTLIST monitor %global_name;
                  location CDATA #REQUIRED
                  baseport CDATA #REQUIRED>
<!ELEMENT probe EMPTY>
<!ATTLIST probe %global_name;>
<!-- End declare system view instances -->
```

3. The DTD for Detection Tasks

```
<!ENTITY % global_name      "name  NMTOKEN #REQUIRED">
<!ENTITY % local_name_def "name  ID #REQUIRED">
<!ENTITY % local_name_ref "name IDREF #REQUIRED">
<!ENTITY % element_choice "(attribute | attr_ref | constant)">
<!ENTITY % attr_type "type (timestamp | int | float | varchar)
    #REQUIRED">
<!ENTITY % attr_len "len NMTOKEN #REQUIRED">

<!ELEMENT task (system_view_inst, partial_match_table,
                timed_condition, parent_node?, child_node*)>
<!ATTLIST task %global_name;
               spec_sig_name NMTOKEN #REQUIRED
               type (positive | negative) "positive"
               root (yes | no) "no">
<!-- Begin system view instances -->
<!ELEMENT system_view_inst (monitor, probe)>
<!ATTLIST system_view_inst %global_name; system_view NMTOKEN
    #REQUIRED)>
<!ELEMENT monitor EMPTY>
<!ATTLIST monitor %global_name;
                  location CDATA #REQUIRED
                  baseport CDATA #REQUIRED>
<!ELEMENT probe EMPTY>
<!ATTLIST probe %global_name;>
<!-- End system view instances -->
<!ELEMENT partial_match_table (PMT_attribute+)>
<!ELEMENT PMT_attribute EMPTY>
<!ATTLIST PMT_attribute %global_name; %attr_type; %attr_len;
                        source (inherit | assign) "assign"
                        source_attr NMTOKEN #IMPLIED>
<!ELEMENT parent_node (monitor)>
<!ATTLIST parent_node %global_name;>
<!ELEMENT child_node (monitor, child_partial_match_table)>
<!ATTLIST child_node %global_name;>
<!ELEMENT child_partial_match_table (child_PMT_attribute+)>
<!ELEMENT child_PMT_attribute EMPTY>
<!ATTLIST child_PMT_attribute %local_name_def; %attr_type; %attr_len;>
<!-- Begin timed condition -->
<!ENTITY % cond "(and | or | not | equal | greater_than | greater_equal
    | less_than | less_equal | not_equal | predicate)">
<!ELEMENT timed_condition %cond;>
<!ELEMENT and (%cond;, %cond;)>
<!ELEMENT or (%cond;, %cond;)>
<!ELEMENT not %cond;>
<!ELEMENT attribute EMPTY>
<!ATTLIST attribute %global_name; %attr_type; %attr_len; >
<!ELEMENT constant EMPTY>
<!ATTLIST constant value CDATA #REQUIRED %attr_type;>
```

```
<!ELEMENT attr_ref EMPTY>
<!ATTLIST attr_ref %local_name_ref;>
<!ELEMENT equal (%element_choice;, %element_choice;)>
<!ELEMENT greater_than (%element_choice;, %element_choice;)>
<!ELEMENT greater_equal (%element_choice;, %element_choice;)>
<!ELEMENT less_than (%element_choice;, %element_choice;)>
<!ELEMENT less_equal (%element_choice;, %element_choice;)>
<!ELEMENT not_equal (%element_choice;, %element_choice;)>
<!ELEMENT predicate (parameter*)>
<!ATTLIST predicate %global_name; time (begin|end|exist|forall)
    #REQUIRED>
<!ELEMENT parameter %element_choice;>
<!-- End timed condition -->
```

Appendix B
Sample System Views, Signatures and Detection Tasks in CARDS

In this appendix, we show some examples of the internal XML representation of system views, signatures, and detection tasks. We assume the DTDs of these XML files are accessible at "http://infosec/".

1. System Views

1.1 The System View *DOSAttacks*

```
<?xml version="1.0" standalone="no" ?>
<!DOCTYPE system_view SYSTEM "http://infosec/sysview.dtd">
<system_view name="GMU:DOSAttacks">
  <event_schema>
    <attribute name="Attack" type="varchar" len="30">
      <possible_value value="SYN_Flooding"/>
      <possible_value value="Tear_Drop"/>
      <possible_value value="Land"/>
    </attribute>
    <attribute name="Protocol" type="varchar" len="5">
      <possible_value value="TCP"/>
      <possible_value value="UDP"/>
      <possible_value value="ICMP"/>
    </attribute>
    <attribute name="VictimIP" type="varchar" len="15"/>
    <attribute name="VictimPort" type="int" len="1"/>
  </event_schema>
  <description>
    The system view DOSAttacks provides an interface for network based
    Denial of Service (DOS) attacks. Currently three types of DOS
    attacks, i.e., SYN flooding attack, Tear Drop, and Land, are
    supported by DOSAttacks. When the attack is based on TCP, both
    VictimIP and VictimPort are valid; when the attack is based on UDP
```

or ICMP, VictimPort should be ignored. VictimIP is expected to be
in the form of "129.174.142.121", and VictimPort should be an
integer (e.g., 21 for the telnet port).
```
  </description>
</system_view>
```

1.2   The System View *LocalTCPConn*

```
<?xml version="1.0" standalone="no"?>
<!DOCTYPE system_view SYSTEM "http://infosec/sysview.dtd">
<system_view name="GMU:LocalTCPConn">
  <event_schema>
    <attribute name="SrcIP" type="varchar" len="15"/>
    <attribute name="SrcPort" type="int" len="1"/>
    <attribute name="DstIP" type="varchar" len="15"/>
    <attribute name="DstPort" type="int" len="1"/>
  </event_schema>
  <description>
```
The system view LocalTCPConn provides an interface for local TCP
connection events. The attributes SrcIP, SrcPort, DstIP, and
DstPort are source IP address, source port number, destination IP
address, and destination port number, respectively. The IP
addresses are expected to be in the form of, say
"129.174.142.121", and VictimPort should be an integer (e.g., 21
for the telnet port).
```
  </description>
</system_view>
```

2.   The Generic Signature for the Mitnick Attack

```
<?xml version="1.0" standalone="no"?>
<!DOCTYPE signature SYSTEM "http://infosec/signature.dtd">
<signature name="mitnick">
  <node name="n1">
    <system_view_inst name="SysView1"/>
    <assignment>
      <variable name = "var_IP"/>
      <attribute name="VictimIP"/>
    </assignment>
    <assignment>
      <variable name="var_Port"/>
      <attribute name="VictimPort"/>
    </assignment>
    <timed_condition>
      <equal>
        <attribute name="Attack"/>
        <constant value="SYN_Flooding"/>
      </equal>
    </timed_condition>
  </node>
```

```
<node name="n2">
  <system_view_inst name="SysView2"/>
  <assignment>
      <variable name="var_SrcIP"/>
      <attribute name="SrcIP"/>
  </assignment>
  <assignment>
      <variable name="var_SrcPort"/>
      <attribute name="SrcPort"/>
  </assignment>
  <assignment>
      <variable name="var_DstIP"/>
      <attribute name="DstIP"/>
  </assignment>
  <assignment>
      <variable name="var_DstPort"/>
      <attribute name="DstPort"/>
  </assignment>
  <timed_condition>
    <and>
        <equal>
            <attribute name="SrcIP"/>
            <var_ref name="var_IP"/>
        </equal>
        <equal>
            <attribute name="SrcPort"/>
            <var_ref name="var_Port"/>
        </equal>
    </and>
  </timed_condition>
</node>
<node name="n3" type="negative">
  <system_view_inst name="SysView3"/>
  <timed_condition>
    <and>
        <equal>
            <attribute name="SrcIP"/>
            <var_ref name="var_SrcIP"/>
        </equal>
        <and>
          <equal>
              <attribute name="SrcPort"/>
              <var_ref name="var_SrcPort"/>
          </equal>
          <and>
            <equal>
                <attribute name="DstIP"/>
                <var_ref name="var_DstIP"/>
            </equal>
            <equal>
```

```
                <attribute name="DstPort"/>
                <var_ref name="var_DstPort"/>
              </equal>
            </and>
          </and>
        </and>
      </timed_condition>
    </node>
    <edge from="n2" to="n1" label="during"/>
    <edge from="n3" to="n2" label="equal"/>
    <declare_sys_view_inst name="SysView1"
       system_view="GMU:DOSAttacks"/>
    <declare_sys_view_inst name="SysView2"
       system_view="GMU:LocalTCPConn"/>
    <declare_sys_view_inst name="SysView3"
       system_view="GMU:LocalTCPConn"/>
</signature>
```

3.   One Specific Signature for the Mitnick Attack

```
<?xml version="1.0" standalone="no" ?>
<!DOCTYPE signature SYSTEM "http://infosec/signature.dtd">
<signature generic_name="mitnick" name="mitnick_inst_1">
  <node name="n1" rare="no" type="positive">
    <system_view_inst name="SysView1"/>
    <assignment>
      <variable name="var_IP"/>
      <attribute name="VictimIP"/>
    </assignment>
    <assignment>
      <variable name="var_Port"/>
      <attribute name="VictimPort"/>
    </assignment>
    <timed_condition>
      <equal>
        <attribute name="Attack"/>
        <constant type="varchar" value="SYN_Flooding"/>
      </equal>
    </timed_condition>
  </node>
  <node name="n2" rare="no" type="positive">
    <system_view_inst name="SysView2"/>
    <assignment>
      <variable name="var_SrcIP"/>
      <attribute name="SrcIP"/>
    </assignment>
    <assignment>
      <variable name="var_SrcPort"/>
      <attribute name="SrcPort"/>
```

```
        </assignment>
        <assignment>
          <variable name="var_DstIP"/>
          <attribute name="DstIP"/>
        </assignment>
        <assignment>
          <variable name="var_DstPort"/>
          <attribute name="DstPort"/>
        </assignment>
        <timed_condition>
          <and>
            <equal>
              <attribute name="SrcIP"/>
              <var_ref name="var_IP"/>
            </equal>
            <equal>
              <attribute name="SrcPort"/>
              <var_ref name="var_Port"/>
            </equal>
          </and>
        </timed_condition>
      </node>
      <node name="n3" rare="no" type="negative">
        <system_view_inst name="SysView3"/>
        <timed_condition>
          <and>
            <equal>
              <attribute name="SrcIP"/>
              <var_ref name="var_SrcIP"/>
            </equal>
            <and>
              <equal>
                <attribute name="SrcPort"/>
                <var_ref name="var_SrcPort"/>
              </equal>
              <and>
                <equal>
                  <attribute name="DstIP"/>
                  <var_ref name="var_DstIP"/>
                </equal>
                <equal>
                  <attribute name="DstPort"/>
                  <var_ref name="var_DstPort"/>
                </equal>
              </equal>
            </and>
          </and>
        </and>
        </timed_condition>
      </node>
      <edge from="n2" label="during" to="n1"/>
```

```
  <edge from="n3" label="equal" to="n2"/>
  <declare_sys_view_inst name="SysView1" system_view="GMU:DOSAttacks">
    <monitor baseport="4200" location="129.174.142.140" name="Kong"/>
    <probe name="SynFloodProbe"/>
  </declare_sys_view_inst>
  <declare_sys_view_inst name="SysView2" system_view="GMU:LocalTCPConn">
    <monitor baseport="4200" location="129.174.142.177" name="Discovery"/>
    <probe name="LocalTCPConn"/>
  </declare_sys_view_inst>
  <declare_sys_view_inst name="SysView3" system_view="GMU:LocalTCPConn">
    <monitor baseport="4200" location="129.174.142.140" name="Kong"/>
    <probe name="LocalTCPConn"/>
  </declare_sys_view_inst>
</signature>
```

4. The Detection Tasks for the Specific Signature of the Mitnick Attack

4.1 Detection Task n_1

```
<?xml version="1.0" standalone="no" ?>
<!DOCTYPE task SYSTEM "http://infosec/task.dtd">
<task name="n1" root="no" spec_sig_name="mitnick_inst_1"
    type="positive">
  <system_view_inst name="SysView1" system_view="GMU:DOSAttacks">
    <monitor baseport="4200" location="129.174.142.140" name="Kong"/>
    <probe name="SynFloodProbe"/>
  </system_view_inst>
  <partial_match_table>
    <PMT_attribute len="1" name="end_time_n1" source="assign"
      source_attr="end_time" type="DateTime"/>
    <PMT_attribute len="1" name="var_Port" source="assign"
      source_attr="VictimPort" type="int"/>
    <PMT_attribute len="15" name="var_IP" source="assign"
      source_attr="VictimIP" type="varchar"/>
    <PMT_attribute len="1" name="begin_time_n1" source="assign"
      source_attr="begin_time" type="DateTime"/>
  </partial_match_table>
  <timed_condition>
    <equal>
      <attribute len="30" name="Attack" type="varchar"/>
      <constant type="varchar" value="SYN_Flooding"/>
    </equal>
  </timed_condition>
  <parent_node name="n2">
    <monitor baseport="4200" location="129.174.142.177"
      name="Discovery"/>
  </parent_node>
</task>
```

4.2   Detection Task n_2

```xml
<?xml version="1.0" standalone="no" ?>
<!DOCTYPE task SYSTEM "http://infosec/task.dtd">
<task name="n2" root="yes" spec_sig_name="mitnick_inst_1"
    type="positive">
  <system_view_inst name="SysView2" system_view="GMU:LocalTCPConn">
    <monitor baseport="4200" location="129.174.142.177"
        name="Discovery"/>
    <probe name="LocalTCPConn"/>
  </system_view_inst>
  <partial_match_table>
    <PMT_attribute len="1" name="var_DstPort" source="assign"
        source_attr="DstPort" type="int"/>
    <PMT_attribute len="15" name="var_SrcIP" source="assign"
        source_attr="SrcIP" type="varchar"/>
    <PMT_attribute len="1" name="end_time_n2" source="assign"
        source_attr="end_time" type="DateTime"/>
    <PMT_attribute len="1" name="end_time_n1" source="inherit"
        type="DateTime"/>
    <PMT_attribute len="15" name="var_DstIP" source="assign"
        source_attr="DstIP" type="varchar"/>
    <PMT_attribute len="1" name="var_SrcPort" source="assign"
        source_attr="SrcPort" type="int"/>
    <PMT_attribute len="1" name="begin_time_n2" source="assign"
        source_attr="begin_time" type="DateTime"/>
    <PMT_attribute len="1" name="begin_time_n1" source="inherit"
        type="DateTime"/>
  </partial_match_table>
  <timed_condition>
    <and>
      <and>
        <equal>
          <attribute len="15" name="SrcIP" type="varchar"/>
          <attr_ref name="var_IP"/>
        </equal>
        <equal>
          <attribute len="1" name="SrcPort" type="int"/>
          <attr_ref name="var_Port"/>
        </equal>
      </and>
      <and>
        <greater_than>
          <attribute len="1" name="begin_time" type="int"/>
          <attr_ref name="begin_time_n1"/>
        </greater_than>
        <less_than>
          <attribute len="1" name="end_time" type="int"/>
          <attr_ref name="end_time_n1"/>
        </less_than>
```

```
      </and>
    </and>
  </timed_condition>
  <parent_node name="n3">
    <monitor baseport="4200" location="129.174.142.140" name="Kong"/>
  </parent_node>
  <child_node name="n1">
    <monitor baseport="4200" location="129.174.142.140" name="Kong"/>
    <child_partial_match_table>
      <child_PMT_attribute len="1" name="end_time_n1"
          type="DateTime"/>
      <child_PMT_attribute len="1" name="var_Port" type="int"/>
      <child_PMT_attribute len="15" name="var_IP" type="varchar"/>
      <child_PMT_attribute len="1" name="begin_time_n1"
          type="DateTime"/>
    </child_partial_match_table>
  </child_node>
</task>
```

4.3 Detection Task n_3

```
<?xml version="1.0" standalone="no" ?>
<!DOCTYPE task SYSTEM "http://discovery/task.dtd">
<task name="n3" root="yes" spec_sig_name="mitnick_inst_1''
    type="negative">
  <system_view_inst name="SysView3" system_view="GMU:LocalTCPConn">
    <monitor baseport="4200" location="129.174.142.140" name="Kong"/>
    <probe name="LocalTCPConn"/>
  </system_view_inst>
  <partial_match_table>
    <PMT_attribute len="1" name="end_time_n3" source="assign"
        source_attr="end_time" type="DateTime"/>
    <PMT_attribute len="1" name="end_time_n2" source="inherit"
        type="DateTime"/>
    <PMT_attribute len="1" name="end_time_n1" source="inherit"
        type="DateTime"/>
    <PMT_attribute len="1" name="begin_time_n3" source="assign"
        source_attr="begin_time" type="DateTime"/>
    <PMT_attribute len="1" name="begin_time_n2" source="inherit"
        type="DateTime"/>
    <PMT_attribute len="1" name="begin_time_n1" source="inherit"
        type="DateTime"/>
  </partial_match_table>
  <timed_condition>
    <and>
      <and>
        <equal>
          <attribute len="15" name="SrcIP" type="varchar"/>
          <attr_ref name="var_SrcIP"/>
        </equal>
```

```xml
          <and>
            <equal>
              <attribute len="1" name="SrcPort" type="int"/>
              <attr_ref name="var_SrcPort"/>
            </equal>
            <and>
              <equal>
                <attribute len="15" name="DstIP" type="varchar"/>
                <attr_ref name="var_DstIP"/>
              </equal>
              <equal>
                <attribute len="1" name="DstPort" type="int"/>
                <attr_ref name="var_DstPort"/>
              </equal>
            </and>
          </and>
        </and>
        <and>
          <equal>
            <attribute len="1" name="begin_time" type="int"/>
            <attr_ref name="begin_time_n2"/>
          </equal>
          <equal>
            <attribute len="1" name="end_time" type="int"/>
            <attr_ref name="end_time_n2"/>
          </equal>
        </and>
      </and>
    </timed_condition>
    <parent_node name="n2">
      <monitor baseport="4200" location="129.174.142.177"
          name="Discovery"/>
    </parent_node>
    <child_node name="n2">
      <monitor baseport="4200" location="129.174.142.177"
          name="Discovery"/>
      <child_partial_match_table>
        <child_PMT_attribute len="1" name="var_DstPort" type="int"/>
        <child_PMT_attribute len="15" name="var_SrcIP" type="varchar"/>
        <child_PMT_attribute len="1" name="end_time_n2"
            type="DateTime"/>
        <child_PMT_attribute len="1" name="end_time_n1"
            type="DateTime"/>
        <child_PMT_attribute len="15" name="var_DstIP" type="varchar"/>
        <child_PMT_attribute len="1" name="var_SrcPort" type="int"/>
        <child_PMT_attribute len="1" name="begin_time_n2"
            type="DateTime"/>
        <child_PMT_attribute len="1" name="begin_time_n1"
            type="DateTime"/>
      </child_partial_match_table>
```

```
  </child_node>
</task>
```

References

[Abrams et al., 1997] Abrams, M. D., Jajodia, S., and Podell, H. J., editors (1997). *Information Security: An Integrated Collection of Essays*. IEEE Computer Society Press.

[Allen, 1983] Allen, J. F. (1983). Maintaining knowledge about temporal intervals. *Communications of the ACM*, 26(11):832–843.

[Anderson et al., 1995] Anderson, D., Lunt, T. F., Javitz, H., Tamaru, A., and Valdes, A. (1995). Detecting unusual program behavior using the statiscal component of the next-generation intrusion detection expert system (NIDES). Technical Report SRI-CSL-95-06, SRI Internal, Computer Science Laboratory.

[Anderson, 1980] Anderson, J. P. (1980). Computer security threat monitoring and surveillance. Technical report, James P. Anderson Co., Fort Washington, PA.

[Barbara et al., 2001a] Barbara, D., J., Cuotuo, Jajodia, S., and Wu, N. (2001a). ADAM: A testbed for exploring the use of data mining in intrusion detection. *ACM SIGMOD Record*, 30(4):15–24.

[Barbara et al., 2001b] Barbara, D., Wu, N., and Jajodia, S. (2001b). Detecting novel network intrusion using bayes estimators. In *Proceedings of the First SIAM Conference on Data Mining*.

[Bray et al., 1998] Bray, T., Paoli, J., and Sperberg-McQueen, C. M. (1998). Extensible markup language (XML) 1.0. W3C Recommendation 10-February-1998.

[BSM,] BSM. *Solaris SHIELD Basic Security Module Revision A*.

[CERT, 1999a] CERT (1999a). Distributed denial of service tools. CERT Incident Note IN-99-07, http://www.cert.org/incident_notes/IN-99-07.html.

[CERT, 1999b] CERT (1999b). Results of the distributed-systems intruder tools workshop. http://www.cert.org/reports/dsit_workshop-final.html.

[Chang et al., 2001] Chang, H., Wu, S.F., and Jou, Y.F. (2001). Real-time protocol analysis for detecting link-state routing protocol. *ACM Transactions on Information and System Security*, 4(1):1–36.

[Cuppens and Ortalo, 2000] Cuppens, F. and Ortalo, R. (2000). LAMBDA: A language to model a database for detection of attacks. In *Proc. of Recent Advances in Intrusion Detection (RAID 2000)*, pages 197–216.

[Curry and Debar, 2001] Curry, D. and Debar, H. (2001). Intrusion detection message exchange format data model and extensible markup language (xml) document type definition. Internet Draft, draft-ietf-idwg-idmef-xml-03.txt.

[Date and Darwen, 1997] Date, C. J. and Darwen, H. (1997). *A Guide to the SQL standard: a user's guide to the standard database language SQL*. Addison Wisley.

[Degioanni et al.,] Degioanni, L., Risso, F., and Viano, P. WinDump: tcpdump for windows. http://netgroup-serv.polito.it/windump/.

[Denning, 1986] Denning, D. E. (1986). An intrusion-detection model. In *Proceedings of 1986 IEEE Symposium on Security and Privacy*, pages 118–131, Oakland, CA.

[DeWitt et al., 1984] DeWitt, D.J., Katz, R.H., Olken, F., Shapiro, L.D., Stonebraker, M.R., and Wood, D. (1984). Implementation techniques for main memory database systems. *SIGMOD Record*, 14(2):1–8.

[Eckmann et al., 2002] Eckmann, S.T., Vigna, G., and Kemmerer, R.A. (2002). STATL: An Attack Language for State-based Intrusion Detection. *Journal of Computer Security*, 10(1/2):71–104.

[Eichin and Rochis, 1989] Eichin, M. and Rochis, J. (1989). With microscope and tweezers: An analysis of the internet worm of november 1988. In *Proceedings of 1989 IEEE Symposium on Security and Privacy*, pages 326–343, Oakland, CA.

[Feiertag et al., 2000a] Feiertag, R., Kahn, C., Porras, P., Schnackenberg, D., Staniford-Chen, S., and Tung, B. (2000a). A common intrusion specification language. http://www.gidos.org/drafts/language.txt.

[Feiertag et al., 2000b] Feiertag, R., Rho, S., Benzinger, L., Wu, S., Redmond, T., Zhang, C., Levitt, K., Peticolas, D., Heckman, M., Staniford, S., and McAlerney, J. (2000b). Intrusion detection inter-component adaptive negotiation. *Computer Networks*, 34:605–621.

[Feinstein et al., 2001] Feinstein, B.S., Matthews, G.A., and White, J.C.C. (2001). The intrusion detection exchange protocol (IDXP). Internet Draft draft-ietf-idwg-beep-idxp-02.txt.

[Forrest et al., 1996] Forrest, S., Hofmeyr, S. A., and Longstaff, T. A. (1996). A sense of self for unix processes. In *Proceedings of 1996 IEEE Symposium on Security and Privacy*, pages 120–128, Oakland, CA.

[Forrest et al., 1994] Forrest, S., Perelson, A.S, Allen, L., and Cherukuri, R. (1994). Self-nonself discrimination in a computer. In *Proceedings of 1994 IEEE Symposium on Security and Privacy*, pages 202–212, Oakland, CA.

[Fox et al., 1990] Fox, K.L., Henning, R.R., Reed, J.H., and Simonian, R.P. (1990). A neural network approach towards intrusion detection. In *Proceedings of 13th National Computer Security Conference*, pages 125–134.

[Freksa, 1992] Freksa, C. (1992). Temporal reasoning based on semi-intervals. *Artificial Intelligence*, 54(1):199–227.

[Frincke et al., 1998] Frincke, D., Tobin, D., McConnell, J., Marconi, J., and Polla, D. (1998). A framework for cooperative intrusion detection. In *Proceedings of the 21st National Information Systems Security Conference*, Crystal City, Virginia.

[Ghosh et al., 1998] Ghosh, A. K., Wanken, J., and Charron, F. (1998). Detecting anomalous and unknown intrusions against programs. In *Proceedings of the 14th Annual Computer Security Applications Conference*, pages 259–267.

[Heberlein et al., 1992] Heberlein, L. T., Mukherjee, B., and Levitt, K. N. (1992). Internetwork security monitor: An intrusion-detection system for large-scale networks. In *Proceedings of 15th National Computer Security Conference*, pages 262–271, Baltimore, MD.

[Ho et al., 1998] Ho, Y., Frincke, D., and Tobin, D. Jr. (1998). Planning, petri nets, and intrusion detection. In *Proceedings of the 21st National Information Systems Security Conference*, Crystal City, Virginia.

[Hochberg et al., 1993] Hochberg, J., Jackson, K., Stallings, C., McClary, J. F., DuBois, D., and Ford, J. (1993). NADIR: An automated system for detecting network intrusion and misuse. *Computers & Security*, 12(3):235–248.

[Hofmeyr et al., 1998] Hofmeyr, S., Forrest, S., and Somayaji, A. (1998). Intrusion detection using sequences of system calls. *Journal of Computer Security*, 6(1):151–180.

[Ilgun, 1993] Ilgun, K. (1993). USTAT: A real-time intrusion detection system for UNIX. In *Proceedings of IEEE Symposium on Security and Privacy*, pages 16–28, Oakland, CA.

[Ilgun et al., 1995] Ilgun, K., Kemmerer, R. A., and Porras, P. A. (1995). State transition analysis: A rule-based intrusion detection approach. *IEEE Transaction on Software Engineering*, 21(3):181–199.

[ITSE, 1991] ITSE (1991). Information technology security evaluation criteria (ITSEC). Commission of the European Communities, Luxembourg. Provisional Harmonized Criteria: Version 1.2.

[Javits and Valdes, 1993] Javits, H.S. and Valdes, A. (1993). The NIDES statistical component: Description and justification. Technical report, SRI International, Computer Science Laboratory.

[Jou et al., 2000] Jou, Y.F., Gong, F., Sargor, C., Wu, X., Wu, S.F., Chang, H.C., and Wang, F. (2000). Design and implementation of a scalable intrusion detection system for the protection of network infrastructure. In *DARPA Information Survivability Conference and Exposition*.

[Kahn et al., 1998a] Kahn,   C.,   Bolinger,   D.,   and   Schnackenberg,   D. (1998a).   Communication   in   the   common   intrusion   detection   framework. http://www.gidos.org/drafts/communication.txt.

[Kahn et al., 1998b] Kahn, C., Porras, P. A., Staniford-Chen, S., and Tung, B. (1998b). A common intrusion detection framework. Submitted to Journal of Computer Security.

[Kemmerer, 1997] Kemmerer, R. A. (1997). NSTAT: A model-based real-time network intrusion detection system. Technical Report TRCS97-18, Reliable Software Group, Department of Computer Science, University of California at Santa Barbara.

[Kendall, 1999] Kendall, K. (1999). A database of computer attacks for the evaluation of intrusion detection systems. Master's thesis, Department of EECS, MIT.

[Ko et al., 1997] Ko, C., Ruschitzka, M., and Levitt, K. (1997). Execution monitoring of security-critical programs in distributed systems: A specification-based approach. In *Proceedings of 1997 IEEE Symposium on Security and Privacy*, pages 175–187, Oakland, CA.

[Kumar, 1995] Kumar, S. (1995). *Classification and Detection of Computer Intrusions*. PhD thesis, Purdue University.

[Kumar and Spafford, 1994] Kumar, S. and Spafford, E. H. (1994). A pattern matching model for misuse intrusion detection. In *Proceedings of the 17th National Computer Security Conference*, pages 11–21.

[Kummar and Spafford, 1995] Kummar, S. and Spafford, E.H. (1995). A software architecture to support misuse intrusion detection. In *Proceedings of the 18th National Information Systems Security Conference*, pages 194–204.

[Lane and Brodley, 1998] Lane, T. and Brodley, C. E. (1998). Temporal sequence learning and data reduction for anomaly detection. In *Proceedings of 5th Conference on Computer & Communications Security*, pages 150–158.

[Lee et al., 2000] Lee, W., Nimbalkar, R.A., Yee, K.K., Patil, S.B., Desai, P.H., T.T., Tran, and Stolfo, S.J. (2000). A data mining and CIDF based approach for detecting novel and distributed intrusions. In *Proceedings of 3rd International Workshop on the Recent Advances in Intrusion Detection*.

[Lee and Stolfo, 1998] Lee, W. and Stolfo, S. J. (1998). Data mining approaches for intrusion detection. In *Proceedings of the 7th USENIX Security Symposium*.

[Lee et al., 1998] Lee, W., Stolfo, S. J., and Mok, K. W. (1998). Mining audit data to build intrusion detection models. In *Proceedings of the 4th International Conference on Knowledge Discovery and Data Mining*, pages 66–72.

[Lee et al., 1999] Lee, W., Stolfo, S. J., and Mok, K. W. (1999). A data mining framework for building intrusion detection models. In *Proceedings 1999 IEEE Symposium on Security and Privacy*, pages 120–132, Oakland, CA.

[Lee and Stolfo, 2000] Lee, W. and Stolfo, S.J. (2000). A framework for constructing features and models for intrusion detection systems. *ACM Transactions on Information and System Security*, 3(4):227–261.

[Lee. and Xiang, 2001] Lee., W. and Xiang, D. (2001). Information-theoretic measures for anomaly detection. In *Proceedings of 2001 IEEE Symposium on Security and Privacy*, pages 130–143, Oakland, CA.

[Lin, 1998] Lin, J. (1998). *Abstraction-Based Misuse Detection: High-level Specifications and Adaptable Strategies*. PhD thesis, George Mason University, Fairfax, VA.

[Lin et al., 1998] Lin, J., Wang, X. S., and Jajodia, S. (1998). Abstraction-based misuse detection: High-level specifications and adaptable strategies. In *Proceedings of the 11th Computer Security Foundations Workshop*, pages 190–201, Rockport, MA.

[Lindqvist and Porras, 1999] Lindqvist, U. and Porras, P. A. (1999). Detecting computer and network misuse through the production-based expert system toolset (P-BEST). In *Proceedings of the 1999 IEEE Symposium on Security and Privacy*, pages 146–161, Oakland, CA.

[McCanne et al.,] McCanne, S., Leres, C., and Jacobson, V. Tcpdump. Lawrence Berkeley National Laboratory, ftp://ftp.ee.lbl.gov/tcpdump.tar.Z.

[Mounji, 1997] Mounji, A. (1997). *Languages and Tools for Rule-Based Distributed Intrusion Detection*. PhD thesis, University of Namur (Belgium).

[Mounji et al., 1995] Mounji, A., Charlier, B.L., Zampuniéris, D., and Habra, N. (1995). Distributed audit trail analysis. In *Proceedings of the ISOC '95 Symposium on Network and Distributed System Security*, pages 102–112.

[New, 2001] New, D. (2001). The TUNNEL profile. Internet Draft draft-ietf-idwg-beep-tunnel-01.txt.

[Ning et al., 2001] Ning, P., Jajodia, S., and Wang, X. S. (2001). Abstraction-based intrusion detection in distributed environments. *ACM Transactions on Information and System Security*, 4(4):407–452.

[Ning et al., 2002] Ning, P., Jajodia, S., and Wang, X.S. (2002). Design and implementation of a decentralized prototype system for detecting distributed attacks. *Computer Communications, Special Issue on Intrusion Detection Systems*, 25(15):1374–1391.

[Northcutt, 1999] Northcutt, S. (1999). *Network Intrusion Detection: An Analyst's Handbook*. New Riders.

[Porras et al., 1998] Porras, P., Schnackenberg, D., Staniford-Chen, S., Stillman, M., and Wu, F. (1998). The common intrusion detection framework architecture. http://www.gidos.org/drafts/architecture.txt.

[Porras and Neumann, 1997] Porras, P. A. and Neumann, P. G. (1997). EMERALD: Event monitoring enabling response to anomalous live disturbances. In *Proceedings of the 20th National Information Systems Security Conference*, National Institute of Standards and Technology.

[Ranum et al., 1997] Ranum, M. J., Landfield, K., Stolarchuk, M., Sienkiewicz, M., Lambeth, A., and Wall, E. (1997). Implementing a generalized tool for network monitoring. In *Eleventh Systems Administration Conference (LISA '97)*.

[Roesch, 1999] Roesch, M. (1999). Snort - lightweight intrusion detection for networks. In *Proceedings of the 1999 USENIX LISA conference*.

[Rose, 2001] Rose, M. (2001). The blocks extensible exchange protocol core. IETF RFC 3080.

[Schuba et al., 1997] Schuba, C. L., Krsul, I. V., Kuhn, M. G., Spafford, E. H., Sundaram, A., and Zamboni, D. (1997). Analysis of a denial of service attack on TCP. In *Proceeding of 1997 IEEE Symposium on Security and Privacy*, pages 208–223, Oakland, CA.

[Sekar et al., 2001] Sekar, R., Bendre, M., Dhurjati, D., and Bollineni, P. (2001). A fast automaton-based method for detecting anomalous program behaviors. In *Proceedings of 2001 IEEE Symposium on Security and Privacy*, pages 144–155, Oakland, CA.

[Sekar et al., 2002] Sekar, R., Gupta, A., Frullo, J., Shanbhag, T., Tiwari, A., Yang, H., and Zhou, S. (2002). Specification-based anomaly detection: A new approach for detecting network intrusions. In *Proceedings of the 9th ACM Conference on Computer and Communications Security (CCS 03)*, pages 265–274.

[Smaha, 1988] Smaha, S. E. (1988). Haystack: An intrusion detection system. In *Proceedings of Fourth Aerospace Computer Security Applications Conference*.

[Snapp et al., 1991] Snapp, S. R., Brentano, J., Dias, G. V., Goan, T. L., Heberlein, L. T., Ho, C., Levitt, K. N., Mukherjee, B., Smaha, S. E., Grance, T., Teal, D. M., and Mansur, D. (1991). DIDS (distributed intrusion detection system) - motivation, architecture, and an early prototype. In *Proceedings of 14th National Computer Security Conference*, pages 167–176, Washington, D.C.

[Spafford and Zamboni, 2000] Spafford, E.H. and Zamboni, D. (2000). Intrusion detection using autonomous agents. *Computer Networks*, 34:547–570.

[Stallings, 1999] Stallings, W. (1999). *SNMP, SNMPv2, SNMPv3, and RMON 1 and 2*. Addison Wesley.

[Staniford-Chen et al., 1996] Staniford-Chen, S., Cheung, S., Crawford, R., Dilger, M., Frank, J., Hoagland, J., Levitt, K., Wee, C., Yip, R., and Zerkle, D. (1996). GrIDS - a graph based intrusion detection system for large networks. In *Proceedings of the 19th National Information Systems Security Conference*, volume 1, pages 361–370.

[Staniford-Chen and Heberlein, 1995] Staniford-Chen, S. and Heberlein, L. (1995). Holding intruders accountable on the internet. In *Proceedings of 1995 IEEE Symposium on Security and Privacy*, pages 39–49, Oakland.

[Teng et al., 1990] Teng, H. S., Chen, K., and Lu, S.C-Y (1990). Adaptive real-time anomaly detection using inductively generated sequential patterns. In *Proceedings of 1990 IEEE Symposium on Security and Privacy*, pages 278–284, Oakland, CA.

[TimesTen Performance Software, 2001] TimesTen Performance Software (2001). Architecture for real-time data management: Timesten's core in-memory database technology. White Paper.

[Tung, 1998] Tung, B. (1998). CIDF APIs: Their care and feeding. http://www.gidos.org/drafts/apis.txt.

[Ullman and Widom, 1997] Ullman, J. and Widom, J. (1997). *A First Course in Database Systems*. Prentice Hall.

[Vigna and Kemmerer, 1999] Vigna, G. and Kemmerer, R. A. (1999). NetSTAT: A network-based intrusion detection system. *Journal of Computer Security*, 7(1):37–71.

[Vigna and Kermmerer, 1998] Vigna, G. and Kermmerer, R. A. (1998). NetSTAT: A network-based intrusion detection approach. In *Proceedings of the 14th Annual Security Applications Conference*.

[Vigna and Kermmerer, 2001] Vigna, G. and Kermmerer, R. A. (2001). Designing a web of highly-configurable intrusion detection sensors. In *Proceedings of the 4th International Symposium on Recent Advances in Intrusion Detection (RAID 2001)*, pages 69–84.

[Wagner and Dean, 2001] Wagner, D. and Dean, D. (2001). Intrusion detection via static analysis. In *Proceedings of 2001 IEEE Symposium on Security and Privacy*, pages 156–168, Oakland, CA.

[Warrender et al., 1999] Warrender, C., Forrest, S., and Pearlmutter, B. (1999). Detecting intrusions using system calls: Alternative data models. In *Proceedings of 1999 IEEE Symposium on Security and Privacy*, pages 133–145, Oakland, CA.

[White et al., 1996] White, G. B., Fisch, E. A., and Pooch, U. W. (1996). Cooperating security managers: A peer-based intrusion detection system. *IEEE Network*, pages 20–23.

[Wu et al., 2000] Wu, S.F., Chang, H.C., Jou, F., Wang, F., Gong, F., Sargor, C., Qu, D., and Cleaveland, R. (2000). JiNao: Design and implementation of a scalable intrusion detection system for the OSPF routing protocol. *Journal of Computer Networks and ISDN Systems*, 34.

Index